F.SCOTT FITZGERALD

F. SCOTT FITZGERALD

BY HOWARD GREENFELD

CROWN PUBLISHERS, INC., NEW YORK

Acknowledgments

It would have been impossible to write this book without the advice and encouragement of my editor, Norma Jean Sawicki. I would also like to thank Beth Greenfeld and Tamara Hovey for their help.

The text of this book is set in 14 point Bodoni Book. The illustrations are black and white photographs, reproduced in halftone.

31009185

To Belle and Abner Sideman

F. SCOTT FITZGERALD

CHAPTER ONE

JUST THE NAME F. SCOTT FITZGERALD CONJURES UP A world of glamour and riches and uninhibited good times. Parties with world-famous guests; flappers; the joys of the reckless Jazz Age. Beauty and brilliance and charm and worldliness. *The good life.* And then Zelda. Just one word that means to the world the devastatingly beautiful, pleasure-seeking wife of a handsome, elegantly dressed writer named F. Scott Fitzgerald.

But they were a tragically unhappy couple, and Scott Fitzgerald was—in almost every way—a failure, no matter how energetically he sought success. He wanted to be a great football player, to score touchdown after touchdown, but he was too small. He wanted to be accepted and admired at a fashionable college, but he didn't have enough money and misunderstood the rules necessary to success at Princeton. Then, he sought fame as a war hero, and his company was never sent overseas into battle. He had a gift and a flair for the theatre, but his plays weren't good enough. He tried to be a snob, but he lacked the wealth and taste in the "right things" that would qualify him to act the snob:

fashion, gourmandise, the ability to say the right thing at the right time.

He wanted to be the ideal husband to the woman he loved, but his wife had an incurable mental illness—and how could he help wonder how much of the fault was his own? He wanted to be the perfect father, and he tried desperately to be one, but circumstances forced him to live apart from his adored daughter much of the time.

He loved the movies and saw films as the vehicle for his talent, but his career as a screenwriter was frustrated at every turn by insensitive producers and directors, by Hollywood itself, and by its code of morals that has long since passed into oblivion.

Above all, he wanted to be a great novelist and short-story writer, and he worked tirelessly toward that goal. He often had commercial success, but only one of his novels sold really well, and what many think would have been his best book was left uncompleted at the time of his death.

Scott Fitzgerald recognized and even foretold his failures, and for the most part he was right. He was not a good football player or playwright; he could not ever have been a war hero or a true snob. He could never work successfully in Hollywood nor was he temperamentally suited to the role of the perfect husband or father. Yet he was wrong when he thought of himself as a failure as a writer. Time has proven him to be one of the most important—and enduring —American writers of the twentieth century.

F. Scott Fitzgerald.

He was born in St. Paul, Minnesota, at three thirty in
the afternoon of September 24, 1896. He was a healthy,
ten-pound six-ounce baby, but an air of anxiety surrounded

Fitzgerald's mother, Mary McQuillan Fitzgerald.

his first months. His parents' two previous children had died in infancy, victims of disastrous epidemics. This newborn child, then, assumed a special importance, requiring more love and more attention.

The name given the child, Francis Scott, came from that of Francis Scott Key, the distinguished American lawyer who wrote "The Star Spangled Banner." Edward Fitzgerald, the baby's father, was in fact descended from the Scotts and the Keys, and this proud heritage was of utmost importance to the Maryland-born Fitzgerald who had left the South after the Civil War to come north and settle in St. Paul. He was a quiet man, a gentle man of great charm and exceptionally good manners, which, together with an unfailing sense of decency, he was able to instill into his son. He was small and dapper and distinguished looking, but he lacked vitality and drive and lived his life constantly in the shadow of his wife.

His wife's shadow was a powerful one. Mary McQuillan is said to have persuaded the handsome Edward Fitzgerald to marry her by threatening to throw herself into the Mississippi River (along which they were walking at the time) unless he proposed marriage—which he did. After all, Mary was almost thirty years old, and it was time for her to marry. The daughter of an Irish immigrant who had made his fortune as a wholesale grocer in St. Paul, Mary, though physically unattractive, managed to exert a strong influence on those around her—including her son. She was an eccentric: she dressed carelessly, often wearing one black shoe and one brown, and her unruly hair went in whichever direction the wind blew it. Rain or shine, she always carried an umbrella. She was a compulsive reader and was frequently seen rushing in or out of the library, but her taste in literature was undiscriminating. She preferred the cheap, romantic works of the time to books of real distinction. A nervous, anxious woman, she was often a source of embarrassment to her courtly, calm husband and later to young Scott. Nonetheless, she had a stubborn determination, as well as a lively imagination, which she passed on to her son. She also had the wealthy background to support the family in their all-too-frequent times of need, since her father, upon his death at the age of forty-four, had left an estate of over a quarter of a million dollars as well as a prospering business. He also left a sumptuous Victorian house in St. Paul's most fashionable section, a home that would represent security to young Scott during his formative years.

When Scott was born, his father was running a small furniture business, but shortly afterward the business failed, and with it all hopes of a calm, steady childhood for the young boy. Edward Fitzgerald found work as a salesman for Procter and Gamble, which meant leaving St. Paul, and until he was twelve years old Scott lived wherever his father's work took him. At first this meant Buffalo, New York, then Syracuse, where his only sister Annabel was born in 1901, and then Buffalo once again. In neither city did the Fitzgeralds manage to establish a home, moving frequently from house to house and neighborhood to neighborhood.

It is perhaps for this reason that the young boy was forced to invent a more stable, inner world of his own. He grew

The house in St. Paul, Minnesota, as it appeared in 1916, when Fitzgerald lived there.

up with a dream of excellence, achievement, and success. At a very early age, he displayed an extraordinarily rich imagination. When he was only five years old, he described his pony so vividly that his grandmother actually believed

Fitzgerald at age three, with his father, Edward Fitzgerald. Christmas 1899.

he had one—which, of course, was not the case. He told convincing tales of the yachts he imagined he owned, fooling mature friends of his family. He read passionately, spending hours in the library, and he emulated and imitated the heroes of the books he read. Physically he was a small child and a fragile one, and for this reason he especially admired those fictional heroes who succeeded in spite of their small size or physical weaknesses, those who achieved their goals in the face of seemingly hopeless odds. Before he was ten years old, he was spending Saturday afternoons at the theatre, rushing home after each performance to put on makeup and improvised costumes, preparing to perform as the actors themselves had.

Because his world was self-created, he insisted upon being the center of it. The people around him were merely secondary characters to whom he assigned roles. However, other children were not always willing—or able—to play the roles given them by Scott. He had decided that he would officially enter society on his sixth birthday, and an elaborate party was planned to celebrate the occasion. Dressed in his neatly pressed sailor suit, his hands scrubbed, his hair plastered down with tonic, he waited for the guests to arrive and pay homage. It was one of his first bitter disappointments: no one came because of a rainstorm, and finally in desperation he ate the entire birthday cake, along with several candles.

His mother encouraged him in his ambitions; she agreed that her beautiful and charming child should be the center of attention. There was no attempt made to discipline him.

At the age of four he was sent to school, but he cried so hard that he was taken out after one day. In Buffalo, he agreed to go to school only on the condition that he could attend half a day. More than that would be a strain. His father was weak and his ideas were of no importance; his mother, who made sure he was the best-dressed child wherever he went, reminded him of his distinguished heritage and encouraged him to believe he was a born leader.

He had no reason to question this until March 1908, when his father was abruptly fired from his job while the family was living in Buffalo. Scott was terrified, frightened that the family would have to go to the poorhouse. For the first time he was aware of money and its insecurities, and he was to be almost obsessed with fear of poverty for the rest of his life.

Fortunately, money was no real problem for the Fitzgeralds, since Mary McQuillan Fitzgerald's family had left enough to provide for their well-being. They might not be rich, but they would be *almost* rich—at least comfortable.

After Edward lost his job, they returned to St. Paul. Scott, then twelve years old, was a lively child, imaginative and dreamy, still anxious to excel in whatever he did. His beautiful manners and appearance—his mother dressed him in Eton collars and silk bow ties—were in his favor. His interests were varied: he collected stamps and organized plays in a neighbor's attic, but his real passions were football and writing. In spite of his size, he played on the neighborhood football team, displaying more enthusiasm than skill, but always working hard. In addition, by the age of twelve he had already written a detective story and started on a history of the United States—though he never got further than the Battle of Bunker Hill. Girls too were beginning to play a part in his life, and he delighted in being one of the stars at the local dancing school, where the boys wore evening pumps and black suits and danced with a handkerchief in their hands. At dancing school, too, his manners and grace won the heart of the much-sought-after Kitty Williams.

He continued to show enormous determination and drive, as well as a need to be the best in all that he undertook. His mother had convinced him that he was "special." When he entered St. Paul Academy in September of 1908, it was these very qualities that made him unpopular with other boys. He was too ambitious and too aggressive, and he had an uncanny—and irritating—ability to see through the people around him, and, to make it even worse, to write about them. He also talked almost compulsively, demanding that attention be paid to him, so much so that an article in the school paper asked if there weren't someone who would "poison Scotty or find some means to shut his mouth."

Classroom work bored him. It seemed a waste of time. While his teachers lectured, he would write stories in the back of his geography book or his Latin book, in the margins of themes and pages filled with declensions and mathematical problems. After class, he kept trying, hopelessly, to excel in sports; a star athlete would necessarily be popular with the other boys. However, he broke a rib while playing football, and the best he could do in baseball was to win a place as second-string pitcher for the academy's third team! But defeats and setbacks never stopped him, and he went on trying harder than ever.

His self-esteem was such that he was never truly discouraged, but it was fortunate for the boy that he was more successful in his other extracurricular activities. His need to hold forth on any subject led to his becoming a star of the debating team, and he became the leader of a club first called the Scandal Detectives and then the Gooserah. Even more important, he continued to write energetically. He wrote detective stories and Civil War stories (it was his tradition-conscious father who encouraged his passion for American history); he wrote football stories, imagining himself as the hero, and he wrote plays.

The more he wrote and the more he gave himself to out-of-school activities, the less he conformed to the requirements of the classroom. His family was worried. His charm and imagination were not enough, and he was clearly in need of more rigid discipline. The only possible solution was to send the boy away to boarding school. He was unusually bright—even his detractors admitted that—but formal schooling was essential to his development.

The school the Fitzgeralds chose was the Newman School,

a small Catholic preparatory school near Hackensack, New Jersey, a forty-minute ride from New York City. Newman catered to boys from well-to-do Catholic families, and its reputation was excellent. There were only about sixty students, which meant that Scott would receive the proper individual attention. An added advantage was that Scott would be in the East. The goal of the "good" families of St. Paul, though proud of their own community, was to send their children East to acquire the proper training and culture to prepare them for national leadership.

Scott was thrilled at the prospect. Many popular books of the time described the romantic life led at boarding school, and he was familiar with them all. In a distinguished eastern school, he would have a chance to attain culture, to expand, to achieve the success he had dreamed of. He was determined to be popular at Newman, to prove himself outstanding in every way.

Before he left for the East in the fall of 1911, he took stock of himself—with extraordinary perception for a fifteen-year-old. For over a year he had kept what he called a "Thoughtbook," filled with frank appraisals of his fellow students, which he kept hidden under his bed. But before leaving St. Paul for Newman, he drew up his own self-appraisal.

His philosophy, he felt, was best described as aristocratic egotism. He believed that he was a fortunate young man, capable of expansion, gifted with both a superior mentality and a facility to make the best of that mentality. His horizons were virtually limitless—though he admitted it was beyond his range to become a mechanical genius.

Physically, he found himself to be handsome, a very good dancer, with athletic possibilities—if not achievements. He had charm and poise and magnetism as well as the ability to dominate others and a subtle fascination for women. He had no doubt that he was talented and very quick to learn.

However, he was perceptive enough to see the other side to his nature. There was within him a latent unscrupulousness, a desire to influence people whether for good or for evil. He admitted he was in some ways cold and capable of cruelty, and that he was fresh and moody. He saw in himself a lack of courage, of self-respect, and of perseverance. And he knew, above all, that he was selfish. Many years later, he wrote to his daughter: *"I didn't know till 15 that there was anyone else in the world except me, and it cost me plenty."*

Bursting with enthusiasm and ambition, endowed with this enviable gift for self-analysis as well as a sensitive understanding of those around him, Scott Fitzgerald arrived at Newman . . . and failed. The school itself was surely not to blame. It fulfilled all his dreams, with its stately ivy-covered main building, handsome adjoining cottages, and a well-equipped gymnasium and athletic fields. The setting was undeniably right for his success, but once again he quickly became one of the most unpopular students at the

Fitzgerald at sixteen.

school. He talked so much that he was considered brash and a show-off. He irritated the other boys by endlessly analyzing them. Even his looks were held against him—he was too pretty. And he was far too small and weak to make his mark as a football player. His lack of discipline in the past, too, worked against him. He seemed incapable of being on time for classes or for meals, and this angered the other students who had conformed to the rules.

Scott's failure to achieve the popularity he so badly wanted disturbed him and made him unhappy, but this unhappiness at Newman was at least partially offset by the excitement at being able to go to the theatre in New York. He had loved writing his own plays at home, or watching local or touring groups, but nothing he had known could compare to the glamour of Broadway. Above all, he thrilled to the lively musical comedies, and his favorite was one called *The Quaker Girl*. He too would write musicals, and he minutely studied the book and lyrics of all those that he could. He read every word of each Gilbert and Sullivan libretto, and filled notebook after notebook with musical comedy ideas of his own. He lived for these exciting afternoons in the theatre and paid less and less attention to his studies, seemingly unaware that they were the primary reason for his being sent to school. Therefore, he was both surprised and hurt when his poor grades resulted in his being denied the privilege of going to New York for the weekends. If he didn't work harder at school, there would be no more theatre for him while at Newman. For the first time in his life, he was taught that he would have to pay a price for his pleasures. His mother's indulgence of his every whim had in no way prepared him for this.

Toward the end of his first year at Newman, Scott once again took stock of himself. He knew that in some way he would have to change in order to achieve the popularity he craved. It was obviously his enormous egotism that was blocking his chances for success at school, and he began to make a conscious effort to become less self-centered and more concerned with the feelings of the other boys. His efforts paid off, and by the time he went home to St. Paul in the late spring, he had improved his position at the school. The first difficult months were behind him.

The summer vacation of 1912 was a good one. With his knowledge of New York theatre, he was able to make a substantial contribution to a St. Paul drama group. Encouraged by this and somewhat more mature because of the problems he had had to face his first year away from home, he returned to Newman in good spirits. He felt that he could make good. Though his real interest was writing, he knew that only success on the football field would assure the needed popularity with the other boys. Because of this, he put all his efforts into the game, and, in spite of his size, he not only made the team but was the star of an important Newman game. His dogged determination had won him a measure of the success he wanted.

Looking back on his days as a schoolboy, Scott Fitzgerald felt his fascination with football had been a mistake, that it had taken his mind off writing. Nonetheless, the time he devoted to football did not prevent him from being an editor for the *Newman News* and writing stories for the newspaper, or from writing musical comedies on his own. Nor did it prevent him from winning a role in the school play or excelling in the school elocution contests. He was, in fact, beginning to fulfill his goals by succeeding at whatever he undertook.

Most important, perhaps, his social and intellectual horizons began to expand through his meeting with a Newman trustee (later to become the school's headmaster) named Father Sigourney Fay. Scott had never met anyone like Father Fay. A wealthy Philadelphian and a convert to Catholicism, Fay was, first of all, extraordinary looking—he was almost pure albino. More important, he was a man of immense charm, intelligence, and magnetism, who had a rare understanding of young people. His understanding of youth led to his realization that in Scott Fitzgerald he had found a young man of unique possibilities. He offered the boy entrée into the world of sophisticated, upper-class eastern Catholics, thereby opening his mind to new ideas and to more profound kinds of literature. He became a kind of father to Scott, and upon his death in 1919, Fitzgerald was heartbroken: *"I can't realize that he has gone,"* he wrote to a friend. *"That all of us who loved him have lost him forever and that that side of life is over, the great warmth and atmosphere that he could cast over youth—the perfect understanding."* Fay's intelligent and compassionate guidance had had such a deep influence on Fitzgerald's early years that for a while after the priest's death Fitzgerald believed that he would become a priest out of his desire to carry on Father's Fay's mission in life.

Near the end of Scott's last year at Newman, the time came to choose a university. It was not a difficult choice. As a child, he had been deeply impressed by a Princeton Glee Club concert. His sense of romance, his sympathy for those who like himself had often barely failed, had made him feel akin to the Princeton football team, which was constantly coming close to winning the championship. And then, as he himself wrote, *"I came across a new musical-comedy score lying on top of the piano. It was a show called* His Honor the Sultan, *and the title furnished the information that it had been presented by the Triangle Club of Princeton University. That was enough for me. From then on the university problem was settled. I was bound for Princeton."*

It wasn't quite that easy. In spite of his excellence in extracurricular activities, Scott's academic record was far from satisfactory. When in May he went to the New York YMCA to take the entrance exams for Princeton, he found he was insufficiently prepared. He failed by a small margin and was advised to study for a makeup exam that would take place in the early fall.

He wanted to go to Princeton, he *had* to go to Princeton, so the hot summer days at home in St. Paul were devoted to long hours of study. In what little spare time he had, he wrote another play for the local drama group. A Civil War drama called *The Coward,* it met with great success and made its young author a celebrity in his hometown. Scott Fitzgerald was known in St. Paul as an interesting young man of great potential. He also became known as a young man who drank. Alcohol somehow excited him; under its influence he felt stronger, more powerful, more able to play the role of the young romantic that he had chosen for himself.

It had been a good summer, but when he went to Princeton in mid-September for his makeup exams, he again failed. However, this time he came so close to passing that he was permitted to appeal his case. The appeal took place on September 24. He was bright and charming and obviously talented—the appeals committee was impressed. In addition, he pointed out the fact that the day on which he pleaded his appeal was his seventeenth birthday; a rejection on such an occasion would be too cruel. In the end, the committee was convinced that Scott Fitzgerald, though not quite up to the mark academically, might make a good Princeton student, and the elated young man proudly sent a telegram to his mother: ADMITTED SEND FOOTBALL PADS AND SHOES IMMEDIATELY PLEASE WAIT TRUNK.

CHAPTER TWO

*"Princeton is in the flat midlands of New Jersey, rising, a
green phoenix, out of the ugliest country of the world. Sor-
did Trenton sweats and festers a few miles south; northward
are Elizabeth and the Erie Railroad and the suburban slums
of New York; westward the dreary upper purlieus of the
Delaware River. But around Princeton, shielding her, is a
ring of silence—certified milk dairies, great estates with pea-
cocks and deer parks, pleasant farms and woodlands. . . .
Two tall spires and then suddenly all around you spreads out
the loveliest riot of Gothic architecture in America, battlement linked on to battlement, hall to hall; arch-broken,
vine-covered—luxuriant and lovely over two square miles of
green grass. Here is no monotony, no feeling that it was all
built yesterday at the whim of last week's millionaire. . . ."*

This is what Scott Fitzgerald wrote ten years after leaving
Princeton and what he must have felt when he first arrived
there. Princeton was more than a university—it was a sym-
bol of conservatism, of wealth, of eastern respectability.
He came to it as a challenger from the Midwest, though,

Aerial view of Princeton University.

admittedly, a worthy challenger. There had been the prelimi-
nary training at Newman among the rich and socially prominent, but Princeton was to be the setting for the real fulfill-
ment of the seventeen-year-old Fitzgerald's dream of fame
and success. When he entered the campus, it seemed to him
that his very life depended upon what happened to him at
the Ivy League school. The important questions, however,
were social. How would he fare among the young men with
the aristocratic names; would he acquire the necessary social
prestige for his future?

Nothing seemed wrong, nothing about Princeton could be
questioned when he first arrived. The college was splendidly
beautiful, and the tradition it evoked even more so. He was

even delighted by the strict rules that applied to all Princeton freshmen: they formed a part of that tradition. Freshmen had to be in their rooms after nine o'clock at night, they were not allowed to walk on the grass as upperclassmen were, they were not allowed to smoke pipes. As for clothing, cuffless trousers were required, as were stiff collars, black ties, shoes and garters, and black skullcaps. To obey these rules made one a Princeton man, and for that reason Scott rigidly adhered to them. In the fall of 1913 Princeton, with its fifteen hundred students, was in the midst of change and expansion, but it still clung to its past, a past which Scott Fitzgerald accepted eagerly.

The surest way to success there, as at most schools and universities, was through football, so once Scott was settled into the rambling stucco rooming house at 15 University Place—along with nine other freshmen, several of them from Newman—he went out for the freshman football team. But, to his bitter disappointment, it was hopeless. The pale, 138-pound, five-foot-seven young man had no chance and lasted just one day. One of his childhood dreams, that of being a famous football star, was finally shattered.

There were, fortunately, other avenues open to him which could lead to his acquiring prestige at Princeton. There was the newspaper, *The Princetonian,* a socially prominent group called the Philadelphian Society, *The Tiger,* a humor sheet, and the nationally known Triangle Club, which had been founded by the author Booth Tarkington and which put on witty musical comedies that annually toured the United States.

Once football was regretfully eliminated, all of Fitzgerald's efforts were directed toward *The Tiger* and the Triangle Club. He flooded the former with short articles, and by sheer persistence persuaded them to publish some of his work. Everything he wrote for Triangle was turned down, but he was undaunted, and in order to become a part of the club he worked on lights for their productions. Putting all his energies into *The Tiger* and Triangle resulted in a dismal start academically—the pattern was repeating itself. Education was once again a secondary matter. Instead of studying algebra and trigonometry, hygiene and coordinate geometry, he thought of articles for the humor sheet and musicals for the drama group. So, at the time of his midterm exams he failed those courses, barely passing his four others. Classwork had bored him—when not writing during lectures, he was sleeping through them—and he was unaware of how dangerous this could be to his overall ambitions at Princeton. Indeed, many beginning Princetonians were expelled each year after poor performances in their midterm examinations. He wasn't expelled, but he came dangerously close, his grades not helped by his taking the maximum number of cuts allowed—forty-nine—during his freshman year.

It didn't matter; he loved Princeton, its atmosphere of wealth and well-being, and when he went home for the Christmas holidays he felt for the first time that St. Paul was too small for him. There were larger worlds for him to conquer.

The conquest began when he returned for his second semester. Triangle was holding its annual competition for an original musical comedy and, urged on by the president of the club, Walker Ellis, Scott worked day and night on his entry for the competition. He was inspired by Gilbert and Sullivan and by Oscar Wilde, whom he studied carefully, but there was a freshness and humor to his writing that was all his own. Though he didn't know it, two other young men destined to be major figures in American literature were also practicing their theatrical talents that year: the graduate student T. S. Eliot and the sophomore e. e. cummings were appearing in a Harvard production of *Fanny and the Servant Problem*.

Fitzgerald's freshman year ended in hope when Triangle accepted the book and lyrics he had written for the finals of their competition. He already knew that his chances of winning were good. If he won, he would be on his way to the success he had dreamed of from early childhood. The Triangle show toured the country each year, playing before audiences in all the major cities of the United States. If chosen, his work would be exposed to the country's most important critics and the public. His disappointment at not making the football team, of not scoring the final winning touchdown, would be almost forgotten. Not completely, however, for Scott Fitzgerald, whatever his triumphs were to be, could never forget and even exaggerated the importance of his failures.

Except for his poor grades—which had improved somewhat during his second semester—his first year at Princeton had been a success. He kept in touch with Father Fay, who visited him and continued to give him wise advice. One of the highlights of Scott's year had been a weekend visit to the home of Father Fay's mother in Deal, New Jersey, where he was able to meet and feel at home with a group of people whose sophistication and worldliness far surpassed that of any group he had ever met. He was stimulated by their conversation and their way of life. Though acutely aware of the difference in his own background, he felt increasingly certain that he could somehow attain the wealth and worldliness that would qualify him to become a part of their circle.

In spite of a nagging feeling that he was a poor boy among the rich, he enjoyed himself. He made friends easily, largely because he was intensely interested in all those around him. He unhesitatingly accepted Princeton's social standards as his own, but he also keenly observed and analyzed them. His off-campus activities his freshman year were pretty much limited to trips to Trenton—to go to burlesque shows and visit bars. But drinking was not socially acceptable at Princeton and drunken behavior was looked on with contempt, so he now limited himself to an occasional beer.

Of all the friends Fitzgerald made during his first year at college, the most important to him was a serious, studious young man named John Peale Bishop. Though four years

John Peale Bishop as a Princeton undergraduate.

older than Scott, Bishop was also a freshman—he had lost
four years of schooling due to a childhood illness. Bishop,
too, was excited about books, and his greater maturity and

his refined literary tastes deeply impressed the younger student, who allowed the warm and generous Bishop to guide him in his reading. Fitzgerald's literary horizons expanded through his friendship with Bishop—who became an important essayist and poet—just as his social horizons broadened throughout his first year at Princeton.

The summer vacation of 1914 was a pleasant one. Scott again worked for the local drama group in St. Paul, this time not only writing but also directing and acting in what was to be a very successful production. In his spare time, he studied hard toward the makeup examinations for the courses he had failed, which awaited him upon his return to Princeton in the fall.

The return was the occasion for both triumph and what he considered to be a tragedy. Triangle had accepted his musical—though Walker Ellis, who had done considerable rewriting on it, took credit for the book, giving Scott credit only for the lyrics. But the Faculty Committee on Non-Athletic Organizations decided that in spite of the improvement in his grades he was academically unsteady and thus ineligible for participation in any Triangle activities. Though his play *Fie! Fie! Fi-Fi!* remained the undisputed winner in the competition, Scott was neither allowed to act in it nor to tour with the production. He was hurt and angry; it seemed to him immensely unjust that the authorities could interfere with his greatest success. What importance were stuffy academic subjects compared to a Triangle musical!

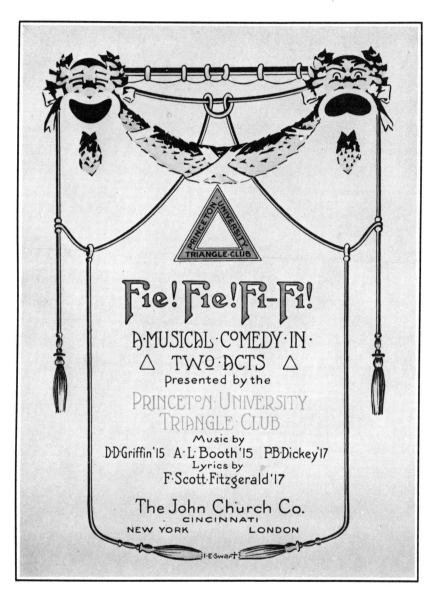

The cover of the musical score Fie! Fie! Fi-Fi! *Fitzgerald wrote the lyrics as well as the book for the Triangle Club's production.*

His experience at Newman was being duplicated at Princeton.

Nonetheless, he helped in every possible way with the production, supervising each detail. *Fie! Fie! Fi-Fi!* was a huge hit at its opening, and Scott's lyrics were cheered. The young author was so pleased with himself that he admitted that he "swelled up like a poison toad." Nonetheless, he could not help feeling sad and bitter when, for the Christmas holidays, the company of his own musical comedy took off for their tour while he returned to St. Paul.

However, he returned to St. Paul a hero. He had made good at Princeton, and word had spread of the success of the Triangle production. He thoroughly enjoyed his new-found prestige, the more so as excellent reviews of the show were sent to him from all over the country. *"Much of the success of the entertainment was due to the clever lyrics of F. S. Fitzgerald,"* wrote the reviewer for the *Baltimore Sun.* *"The lyrics of the songs were written by F. S. Fitzgerald,"* said the critic for the *Louisville Post, "who could take his place right now with the brightest writers of witty lyrics in America."*

His reputation was almost made through his hard work for Triangle. Another form of success and acceptance was within his grasp when, on January 4, at a dinner at the St. Paul Town and Country Club, Scott Fitzgerald met the girl he referred to many years later as *"the first girl I ever loved."*

He had always idealized and romanticized women, and in Ginevra King he found all those qualities that he thought important. Just over sixteen years old, Ginevra had come to St. Paul to visit her friend Marie Hersey. Marie and Ginevra were roommates at the fashionable Westover School in Connecticut. Ginevra was strikingly beautiful, the daughter of a wealthy Chicago family; Marie thought that the handsome and charming Scott would be the perfect match for her.

She was right. In addition to her extraordinary beauty, Ginevra had other qualities that greatly appealed to Scott. She was daring and adventurous, and, above all, she was poised and socially at ease in the upper-class world of wealth to which Scott so avidly sought admittance. What made her even more attractive in the young man's eyes was the fact that she—for the moment at least—chose him over the many men who courted her. Scott Fitzgerald fell deeply in love with this sixteen-year-old beauty, and he was never to forget her; until the time of his death, he kept every letter that she had ever written him.

Their correspondence started upon his return to Princeton the day after their first meeting. Scott's letters were passionate and possessive; she was *his* girl. He had committed himself to her, and for him commitment—whether it be to football or to Triangle—was all-powerful. Ginevra, too, was enthusiastic in her feelings toward the young man, but she was unable to convince him that he was the only man in her

Ginevra King.

life. His jealousy showed in his letters, in spite of Ginevra's assurances that he was very much her favorite. She invited him to visit her at Westover, and though their date was closely supervised by a chaperone—they were too young to be left alone—she was delighted with his witty and charming company, so much so that she suggested they write to each other daily. However, he was still unsure of himself, shaken with fears over the possible end to their love, nagging her on moral issues, and lecturing her pompously in his letters.

Scott's fear of failure with Ginevra—and with the world of wealth she represented—is especially difficult to understand since the spring semester of his sophomore year was the time of his greatest successes at Princeton. For a Princeton student, social success depended upon his acceptance by a proper club. There were eighteen of these clubs, each taking about twenty-five students—which accounted for seventy-five percent of each class. These clubs were all-powerful, the absolute symbols of social achievement. It was at his club that a student ate, invited his girl for weekends, and played billiards with his equals. A student's status was measured by the club to which he belonged. It was, of course, a false measure and a snobbish one, but the tradition was deeply entrenched at Princeton. Though Scott himself recognized the inequities of the situation, while at Princeton his desire was to conform in every way and acceptance of the system of clubs was one way. He wanted, above all, to become the ideal Princeton man, and the ideal Princeton man belonged to one of the top clubs. The period of waiting for a bid from one of these clubs was an anxious one in the life of most students, but Scott's anxieties were quickly put aside. He was offered membership in several clubs, finally choosing the prestigious Cottage Club, to which only the top few were invited.

His membership in Cottage assured him one kind of success, and other triumphs were to follow. He was elected to the office of secretary of Triangle and to the editorial board of *The Tiger*. He was getting to be known as a promising writer, and his writings were published by the *Nassau Lit,* whose editor, Edmund Wilson, became as important to Scott's literary career as was John Peale Bishop. Wilson, who became one of America's most distinguished literary critics, was in many ways Fitzgerald's opposite. It is a tribute to both men's independence and understanding that they became close friends. Wilson was scholarly in a way Fitzgerald could never be. His intellectual gifts were far greater than were Scott's. While Scott participated avidly in all of Princeton's social activities, Wilson was socially withdrawn and ill at ease, vigorously opposing the university's rigidly conservative social structure—the same structure that Scott conformed to enthusiastically. Wilson felt nothing but disdain for Princeton's senseless emphasis on football and clubs and showed interest in neither. Nonetheless, each young man found in the other qualities to be admired. Wilson was drawn

Edmund Wilson as a Princeton undergraduate.

to Fitzgerald's quick imagination and creative spark and encouraged him in every way with his writing. For Scott, Wilson's intellectual standards were impeccable and he listened to him with respect and admiration.

While things were going well for Fitzgerald at Princeton, there were still problems with Ginevra. The romance, because of Scott's nearly hysterical jealousy, was a stormy one —largely by correspondence. He invited her to the sophomore prom, but she was unable to accept because her mother was not free to chaperone her. His letters became unreasonably angry and bitter. He insisted that she was everything to him, while for her he was merely one of many. Finally, he worked himself up to such a state that he wrote Ginevra that he was tired of her, that she was without character, and that he had been wrong to idealize her from the beginning. She calmed him—pointing out that she had never asked to be idealized, and they had a reunion in New York in June when they went to the theatre and danced at the Ritz Roof. She was, he understood from the happy time they spent together, still his girl: but they had spent only a total of fifteen hours together since the day they had first met.

By the time Scott returned to Princeton for his junior year, he seemed well on the way to his hoped-for success. The romance with Ginevra had cooled somewhat over the summer, most of which he spent vacationing at a classmate's ranch in Wyoming, but future glory at Princeton seemed assured. He worked hard for *The Tiger*, more and more of his writings were accepted by the *Nassau Lit*, and his election as secretary of Triangle seemed a sure step toward the presidency of the club. He was enjoying himself, making friends of all kinds, from campus intellectuals to football heroes—he enthusiastically admired excellence and achievement in all areas. He vigorously took part in late-night discussions of pragmatism or the immortality of the soul, and he found equal excitement in the Saturday football games. He loved to go to New York for tea dances at the Plaza or long lunches at Sherry's. The world was his, and he liked it, just as he liked the people who inhabited it. Life's challenges and its infinite possibilities stimulated him—through his writing, he would celebrate its wonders.

Unfortunately, in his enthusiasm he had forgotten once again the ordinary disciplines that were essential for a college student. He had neglected his classwork to such an extent that the same committee that had previously barred him from official participation in extracurricular activities struck him down once again. He was now permanently ineligible for leadership or official participation in any activity beyond the classroom. They made it clear to him that the purpose of Princeton was education.

His dream had been shattered, that dream of crowning his last years at Princeton with glory. However, the fault was his own, and he was forced to accept the decision. He was deeply hurt and angry, but he went on working hard—unofficially—for *The Tiger* and Triangle. He knew college could never be the same, however, and his bitterness over the deprivations caused by his poor grades only served to make those grades poorer. College life no longer made any sense to him so that when he was sent to the infirmary in

November with what was diagnosed as malaria, he withdrew from his activities with indifference. In December, he took a leave of absence from Princeton: the disease was his excuse, but the knowledge that he would again fail his exams was the real reason. He went home to St. Paul a saddened young man and returned to Princeton in February, hoping then to make up for his failed exams. Instead, he was told he would have to redo his entire junior year, beginning the following fall.

The eight months spent in St. Paul before his return to college were wasted. Living at home again bored him. With a few years of living in the East behind him, he found his mother's eccentricities more irritating than ever: her ways embarrassed him. He did a little work for the St. Paul drama group, he occasionally got drunk at parties to soften the effects of his failure, but the time passed slowly. He became filled with a bitterness from which he never fully recovered. Many years later he still remembered what he considered his unfair treatment at the hands of the Princeton authorities and wrote:

"I had lost certain offices, the chief one was the presidency of the Triangle Club, a musical comedy idea, and also I dropped back a class. To me college would never be the same. There were to be no badges of pride, no medals, after all. It seemed on one March afternoon that I had lost every single thing I wanted . . .

"A man does not recover from such jolts—he becomes a different person and, eventually, the new person finds new things to care about."

If Scott Fitzgerald seems to exaggerate the importance of his "failure," this very exaggeration is an indication of how desperately important it was for him to succeed. And when he did return to Princeton, he really was in many ways a new person who had found new things to care about. The new interests, however, were not to be found in the classroom, and his courses bored him more than ever, since for the most part he was repeating subjects he had failed in the past. He found the professors dull and stodgy. They put too much emphasis on the past and were too little concerned with the present and future of the arts. The one exception Scott found to this conservative faculty was a professor of romance languages, Christian Gauss, a man of imagination and sensitivity who was a source of inspiration to his many students, among them Fitzgerald. Gauss became his hero, and the professor was perceptive enough to recognize those qualities which set the embittered young man apart from his fellow students. Perhaps if more members of the Princeton faculty had been able to stimulate Fitzgerald as Gauss had, his college career would have ended differently.

Extracurricular activities were barred to him, and he found little interest in the classroom; as a result, all the passion and energy that he had put into Triangle and into making a social success of his college years was channeled into literature. It showed above all in his writing for the *Nassau Lit;* his stories were more and more serious attempts to understand all that he felt and saw around him and to evaluate his experiences. In addition, he turned to poetry. *"I had decided,"* he wrote later, *"that poetry was the only thing worth while, so with my head ringing with the metres of Swinburne and the matters of Rupert Brooke I spent the spring doing sonnets, ballads and rondels into the small hours. I had read somewhere that every great poet had written great poetry before he was twenty-one."*

Fitzgerald was not writing great poetry, but his attempts at it were tremendously useful to his style since the writing of poetry demanded a discipline in the use of language which he had never practiced before. Once again, his friend John Peale Bishop's influence was great. *"It isn't something easy to get started on by yourself,"* Fitzgerald wrote. *"You need, at the beginning, some enthusiast who also knows his way around—John Peale Bishop performed that office for me at Princeton. I had always dabbled in 'verse' but he made me see, in the course of a couple of months, the difference between poetry and non-poetry. After that one of my first discoveries was that some of the professors who were teaching poetry really hated it and didn't know what it was about. I got in a series of endless scraps with them so that finally I dropped English altogether."* Fitzgerald's disillusion with formal studies was, it seems, complete just as his passion for writing was confirmed.

At the same time, another one of his dreams was shattered —his romance with Ginevra King came to an end. It was finally clear that she was unable to return his undivided devotion, that she was not yet ready to commit herself to one man alone. However, Scott interpreted it in another way, believing that his lack of wealth and true social standing made it impossible for him ever to enter Ginevra's world of fine breeding and money. Poor boys, he had once been told, just shouldn't marry rich girls, and he bitterly concluded that this must be true.

The summer of 1917 was a calm one, and Scott spent much of his time at the home of John Peale Bishop in West Virginia. A few months before—in April—the United States had entered World War One, so much of the talk during that summer centered on the battles raging in Europe and the role that Scott and his friends would play in the war. His personal disappointment with college and the possibilities for change and romance that the war seemed to offer led Fitzgerald to take an examination for a provisional appointment as a second lieutenant toward the end of the summer. The commission came through on October 26, shortly after he had returned to Princeton for what should have been his senior year. His college career thus came to an end, and he enthusiastically reported to infantry officers' training camp at Fort Leavenworth, Kansas, on November 3. He was excited: he had failed to become a football star, but he now had a chance to show his physical strength and courage by becoming a war hero.

First, however, he had to finish a novel on which he had been working. It was to be called *The Romantic Egotist,* and Father Fay, to whom he had shown the manuscript, thought it was excellent. However, Christian Gauss, whom Fitzgerald had asked to send it to his own publisher, Scribner's, felt the novel needed much serious revision before it should be submitted for publication.

So it was that Fitzgerald, handsomely dressed in a made-to-order uniform from the fashionable Brooks Brothers store in New York, arrived at Fort Leavenworth ready and eager to be a hero—after finishing the revisions of his novel. Kansas was a long way from Princeton, and his ivy-covered college dormitory a long way from the room he shared with fifteen other soldiers at Fort Leavenworth. The adjustment was not easy, and his comrades thought him spoiled and soft. The captain in charge of their platoon was a twenty-seven-year-old named Dwight D. Eisenhower, whose promise was greater than Scott's.

Though he wasn't suited to the role, Fitzgerald felt he had to be a war hero—though he didn't like war—just as he had wanted to be a football hero—though he never really liked football. There was, however, a problem: the army interfered with his novel, and he was so bored with the lectures that he spent his time writing instead of listening to what his superiors said. Time and again he was caught and punished, but he kept on writing the novel he referred to as *"a somewhat edited history of me and my imagination."*

As had happened at Newman and at Princeton, he was not following the rules. The reason for going to Newman had not been to enable him to go to the theatre in New York. He was not sent to Princeton in order to excel at extracurricular activities. And he had not joined the army in order to write his novel. Nonetheless, the novel did come first.

Weekends provided his only real time to work. Every Saturday afternoon at one he would rush to the officers' club where, in spite of the smoke-filled room, the rattling newspapers, and the sounds of conversation, he wrote furiously in his notebook until midnight, the club's closing time. He worked even harder on Sundays—from six in the morning until six at night. He had to finish his novel before getting seriously involved in the business of war. *"I had only three months to live—in those days all infantry officers had only three months to live—and I had left no mark on the world,"* he wrote, ironically, years later. Heroism would have to wait.

During three months of weekends, Scott Fitzgerald wrote one hundred and twenty thousand words of his novel, a remarkable feat, another demonstration of his determination. He was sure of himself and wrote to a friend: *"Did you ever notice that remarkable coincidence? Bernard Shaw is 61 years old, H. G. Wells is 51, G. K. Chesterton 41, you're 31 and I'm 21—all the great authors of the world in arithmetical progression. . . . "* As he finished each chapter he sent it off to a typist in Princeton. By March 1918, it was ready to be sent to Shane Leslie, the same friend to whom he had written the above letter. Leslie was more enthusiastic about the book than Christian Gauss had been and he proofread it for corrections and sent it on to Scribner's. He begged the New York publisher not to reject it coldly—the young author was about to go off to die in the war, and it was best that he go to battle feeling that his words would be immortal no matter what happened to him.

However, Fitzgerald was not to go off to war. He joined the Forty-fifth Infantry Regiment in Kentucky and then in Georgia. For a while he was indifferent; the important thing was that his novel was finished. But soon the time for romantic heroism returned. *"The war could go on now,"* he wrote. *"I forgot paragraphs and pentameters, similes and syllogisms."*

In June, he arrived at Camp Sheridan, Alabama. He was a proud if incompetent first lieutenant, assigned to a headquarters company, which entitled him to wear boots and spurs. Again feeling he must look the role he played, he bought yellowish boots, the only officer in the company to do so. It didn't matter if other officers laughed.

However, he was restless, waiting for word from Scribner's about his novel, and he missed the past. He wrote to a friend in June: *"I believe for the first time in my life I'm rather lonesome down here—not lonesome for family and friends or anyone in particular but lonesome for the old atmosphere. . . ."*

His loneliness was soon to come to an end.

CHAPTER THREE

Camp Sheridan was located near the city of Montgomery, Alabama; its population of forty thousand was proud to be Southern and was thus somewhat hostile to the invasion of so many Yankee soldiers at the nearby army camp. Nonetheless, Southern hospitality being what it is, all the officers at Camp Sheridan were invited to the weekly dances given at Montgomery's country club.

It was at one of these dances that Scott Fitzgerald met Zelda Sayre. He was a handsome figure in his neatly tailored Brooks Brothers uniform. Lean and pale and elegant, he stood out among the other soldiers. He was suffering from the news of the marriage of Ginevra King to John Pirie, a wealthy Chicagoan, and this look of suffering made him even more attractive.

He spotted her dancing with a friend of his, Major Dana Palmer. She was startlingly beautiful, with long golden hair and a fresh pink-and-white complexion. In her frilly dress the eighteen-year-old girl was the picture of the Southern belle. Fitzgerald was overwhelmed, all the more so when he spoke to her. She was different from the other girls he had known: she had magic, she was wild and free and wonderfully alive. Her mother had named her Zelda after a gypsy queen, and she lived up to her name. The daughter of a staid, straitlaced judge of the city court of Montgomery, there was nothing in her heritage that could account for her open rebellion against the respectability of her family. As a child, she loved showing off at dancing school, and at high school her interest turned to the drama. She openly defied her parents' conventional values and, because of her charming femininity and beauty, she got away with unheard-of pranks. As a teen-ager, she smoked and drank—things no serious girl of the period ever did. The arrival of so many soldiers at Camp Sheridan gave her the opportunity to meet men from all over the country. Few could resist her, and she delighted at being the center of attention at every country club dance.

Zelda Sayre wanted something special out of life—instinctively she knew there was a more exciting world beyond the confines of Montgomery—just as Scott Fitzgerald did. Their personalities and their ambitions coincided, and they fell deeply in love. Fitzgerald, always the romantic, committed himself as profoundly to Zelda as he had to Ginevra, and once again a woman's commitment was not as all-encompassing as was his. Zelda was unwilling or unable to give up the attentions paid to her by the many soldiers who sought her, and once again Scott found himself involved in stormy, unreasonable quarrels caused by his jealousy. Even with Zelda—not at all Ginevra's social equal—he felt insecure.

F. Scott Fitzgerald and Zelda Sayre outside the Sayres' house in Montgomery, Alabama, 1919.

Zelda knew what she wanted, and she believed that eventually Fitzgerald could provide the life she had envisioned for herself. But that life required success—financial as well as social—and Scott first had to prove himself. He spoke of his literary triumphs at Princeton, of his passion to be a great writer, but Zelda needed concrete evidence. In August, Scribner's returned his novel, *The Romantic Egotist*. They liked it, but their opinion was that it needed extensive revisions, which they urged him to make before resubmitting it for consideration. By October he had revised it according to the publisher's suggestions, but it was finally turned down, only one of their editors, Maxwell Perkins, favoring its acceptance.

There was still no proof that he would become a well-known writer, so at the end of October he hoped he might have a chance to prove to Zelda that he was at least a war hero. His division was ordered overseas. The drama was intense, and he played his role of a soldier about to die with all his theatrical flair. The division was sent to Camp Mills on Long Island, New York, preparatory to crossing the ocean toward the battlefield. After Camp Mills, they entrained to Quebec, a step closer to the field of action. But they were abruptly taken off the train—the war was ending. On November 11, the armistice agreement was signed. Scott Fitzgerald had missed another experience; he would not become a war hero.

The division was returned to New York; it was a period of restlessness and uncertainty. Fitzgerald had too much time on his hands, and he began to drink, as he had occasionally in the past. It seemed to lessen his failures, but he was never able to hold his liquor. With a few drinks he became rude and disagreeable, completely out of control. There were a series of wild parties and his antics began to get him into trouble. He didn't know where he stood as a writer and was uncertain of his future with Zelda. The more he thought about it, the more he drank. He was caught drunk in a hotel room with a naked girl; when his unit was ordered back to Camp Sheridan, he took another route and turned up in

Washington with a girl on each arm and a bottle in his hand.

Once back at Camp Sheridan, he spent every moment he could with Zelda. They were happy together, but the beautiful and popular Southern girl still wasn't sure enough of his ability to support all her whims and extravagances to make a permanent commitment.

For this reason, Fitzgerald went to New York as soon as he was discharged from the army in February 1919. There he would live among the intellectuals and talented bohemians in Greenwich Village. He would take advantage of all the great and glamorous city had to offer and make the money needed to persuade Zelda to marry him. On his arrival in New York he sent her a telegram filled with hope: DARLING HEART AMBITION ENTHUSIASM AND CONFIDENCE I DECLARE EVERYTHING GLORIOUS THIS WORLD IS A GAME AND WHILE I FEEL SURE OF YOUR LOVE EVERYTHING IS POSSIBLE I AM IN THE LAND OF AMBITION AND SUCCESS AND MY ONLY HOPE AND FAITH IS THAT MY DARLING HEART WILL BE WITH ME SOON.

He was twenty-two years old and sure of conquering New York and meeting all its challenges. With proof of his ability in his briefcase—short stories and lyrics for Triangle—he applied for a job as a reporter on each of New York's seven newspapers. All turned him down, and he didn't know why. *"They decided definitely and irrevocably by the sound of my name on a calling card that I was absolutely unfitted to be a reporter,"* he speculated.

The only job open to him was at the Barron Collier Advertising Agency, writing slogans for trolley car cards. His greatest success was one written for a steam laundry in Muscatine, Iowa: "We keep you clean in Muscatine." This piece of poetry brought praise from his boss, who told him that the slogan was "a bit imaginative" but still predicted a good future in advertising for the young man.

Fitzgerald spent nights and weekends writing—stories, sketches, movie scripts, and poems. He worked not in the dreamed-of Greenwich Village apartment, but in a small, stuffy apartment in the Bronx. It was all he could afford on the ninety dollars per month paid him by the advertising agency. Between April and June he wrote nineteen stories, the quickest one in an hour and a half and the slowest in three days. Within a three-month period, there were one hundred and twenty-two rejection slips hanging on the walls of his apartment. He had not even had the satisfaction of a single encouraging letter from an editor.

Socially, he kept up his contacts with his wealthy friends from Princeton. He would spend a Saturday afternoon in the elegant Red Room of the Plaza, go to fashionable garden parties or drink with Princetonians at the bar of the Biltmore Hotel. But, he later remembered, *"I was haunted always by my other life—my drab room in the Bronx, my square foot of the subway, my fixation upon the day's letter from Alabama—would it come and what would it say?—my shabby suits, my poverty, and love."*

His love was not going smoothly. Zelda was increasingly

impatient, wondering how long she would have to wait until her man achieved the promised success. She loved him, but she knew she was temperamentally unfit to endure the hardships of a wife of a struggling writer. Her attitude was not selfish or cruel—it was honest and realistic. She needed glamour and excitement, and it seemed that Scott Fitzgerald would be unable to provide them. Even the sale of his first story to *Smart Set*, a prestigious magazine edited by H. L. Mencken and George Jean Nathan, had its discouraging side —it had been written originally for the *Nassau Lit* two years before. Was it possible that his writing had actually deteriorated since that time?

In June, Fitzgerald went to Montgomery to plead for Zelda's patience and her promise of marriage. She refused, and a violent argument ensued. He was petulant, angry, and self-pitying. In the end, Zelda broke off their informal engagement.

Fitzgerald returned to New York heartbroken. *"I've done my best and I've failed,"* he wrote to a friend. *"It's a great tragedy to me and I feel I have very little left to live for. . . . Unless someday she will marry me I will never marry."*

With Zelda temporarily out of his life, everything seemed useless. He gave up his dull job and for several weeks spent his time drinking. While drinking he could forget, but while drinking he was unable to write. When the drinking bout came to an end, he knew that something positive had to be done. Once again, his powers of self-perception saved him.

He had gone through the little money he had had, and, he realized, for his own well-being and in order to win back Zelda, he had to go on with his novel. He made up his mind to go back to St. Paul, live once again with his parents, and put all his energies into completing the book. His mother had wanted him to make a career in the army, and his father hoped he would go into a respectable business, but they agreed to support him while he worked on his book.

On the Fourth of July, tired and discouraged but still determined, Scott left New York for St. Paul. Once there, his discomfort at again being totally dependent on his parents for support drove him forward. He worked day and night in a small attic room, and by July 26 he wrote to Maxwell Perkins, the Scribner's editor who had originally encouraged him, that he had finished the first draft of a novel called *The Education of a Personage.* *"It is in no sense a revision,"* he said, *"of the ill-fated* Romantic Egotist *but it contains some of the former material, improved and worked over, and bears a strong family resemblance besides."*

On September 4, the completed manuscript was sent to Perkins. By the middle of September, remarkably fast time for a publisher, a special delivery letter came from Perkins saying that Scribner's would publish Fitzgerald's book. It was a courageous move on the part of Perkins, one of America's greatest editors. Scribner's was a solid, conservative house, not truly sympathetic to the works of young, innovative writers. None of the popular authors of the time—

Maxwell Perkins.

Sherwood Anderson, whose *Winesburg, Ohio* was published in 1919; James Branch Cabell, whose *Jurgen* was published the same year; or Sinclair Lewis, who was enjoying his first successes—was on the Scribner list. *"This book is so different,"* Perkins wrote to his new author, *"that it is hard to prophesy how it will sell, but we are all for taking a chance and supporting it with vigor."*

Fitzgerald was ecstatic; he ran up and down Summit Avenue, shouting out the news to all who would listen. *"Of course I was delighted to get your letter,"* he wrote Perkins, *"and I've been in a sort of trance all day; not that I doubted you'd take it but at last I have something to show people."*

Of course, the person he most wanted to impress was Zelda. In his own mind, he had coupled the publication of his novel with her willingness to marry him, and he urged Perkins to bring out his book as soon as possible: *"Would it be utterly impossible for you to publish the book Xmas—or, say, by February? I have so many things dependent on its success—including of course a girl—not that I expect it to make me a fortune but it will have a psychological effect on me and all my surroundings and besides open up new fields."*

Exhilarated, Fitzgerald went back to work with more energy than ever, and he soon found that word of the forthcoming publication of his novel opened up far greater chances for magazine publication. In two months he wrote eight stories and sold nine—the ninth was an old one which was accepted by a magazine that had rejected it four months before. He had not yet earned much money—the magazines to which he sold paid poorly—but in November he was ready to go to Montgomery to convince Zelda to marry him. He proudly presented his case, and she agreed to marry him as soon as his novel, now called *This Side of Paradise*, was published.

When he returned to New York, he moved from his sad apartment in the Bronx to the far more fashionable Knicker-bocker Hotel in Manhattan. He also found a literary agent to sell his writing—Harold Ober of Paul R. Reynolds and Son, who almost immediately sold a story of his to *The Saturday Evening Post* for four hundred dollars. He was elated; this was his first break in a commercial magazine, which would give him a wide public and also pay far greater sums than he had ever been paid. Ober continued to sell his work, and finally Metro-Goldwyn-Mayer, a large Hollywood studio, made an offer to buy one of his stories, "Head and Shoulders," for the movies. What further proof was needed that he was well on the way to success! News of each sale was jubilantly conveyed to Zelda by telegram.

The excitement was too much for him—so much good news after a seemingly hopeless struggle. He celebrated by drinking, but his drinking passed the point of celebration. In a drunken state, he was found tossing twenty- and fifty-dollar bills around his hotel room. What was money when he would soon have so much of it? And he almost flooded the Knickerbocker Hotel by leaving the water running in his bathroom. He could not cope with success.

Obviously, it was time for him to leave New York and return to the relative calm of St. Paul. He arrived there in what he described to Perkins as a "thoroughly nervous alcoholic state." Nonetheless, he was able to pull himself together, and once there he worked feverishly. In a period of four days, he rewrote two stories that had been previously rejected and within a short time received a thousand dollars for them from the *Post*. With that money in hand, he decided to go to New Orleans. He feared that his health was deteriorating and hoped that a period of time in the Southern city would bring about a recovery.

He was worried, too, about the direction his writing was taking. He wrote the short stories with facility, and Ober had no difficulty selling them, but he was somewhat bored with them and eager to get started on a new novel. Thus began a conflict that would be with him for the rest of his life between what he considered good literary work, which satisfied his artistic needs but brought in little money, and the slick commercial writing he was forced to do to earn a living. In New Orleans he wanted to write a serious novel, but he didn't want to be interrupted by preoccupations over money.

Unfortunately, the New Orleans stay was not successful. He was, in spite of himself, constantly worried about his financial future. Understandably, too, he was concerned with the forthcoming publication of his novel, fretting over every detail, from advertising copy to jacket design, from proper typeface to proof corrections. As a result, the novel on which he was working went badly and finally had to be abandoned.

No matter how dissatisfied he felt, his stories did sell and he was beginning to be spoken of in literary circles, so he had no difficulty in convincing Zelda to formalize their engagement in the course of a visit to Montgomery in January 1920. When he returned to New York, more good news awaited him: the movie sale of "Head and Shoulders" was completed. Money seemed to be coming in from all sides, and he celebrated the only way he knew—by drinking too much.

He felt that any celebration was justified. After all, two of his dreams were coming true simultaneously. His novel would be published, and he would marry the woman he loved. His friends shared his delight over the former, but warned him against his union with Zelda. They thought she was too ambitious, too undisciplined and headstrong for him, but they argued to no avail. Fitzgerald defended her to a friend:

"No personality as strong as Zelda's could go without getting criticism. I've always known that any girl who gets stewed in public, who frankly enjoys and tells shocking stories, who smokes constantly and makes the remark that she has 'kissed thousands of men and intends to kiss thousands more,' cannot be considered beyond reproach even if above it. . . .

I fell in love with her courage, her sincerity and her flaming self respect. . . . I love her and that's the beginning and end of everything."

On March 20, Judge and Mrs. Sayre officially announced the engagement of their daughter to F. Scott Fitzgerald, and the proud bridegroom-to-be sent Zelda her first orchid. It was decided that the wedding would take place in New York; only the exact date, after the March 26 publication of *This Side of Paradise,* was uncertain. Before leaving for the big city, Zelda wrote a final letter to her fiancé. *"Darling Heart, our fairy tale is almost ended, and we're going to marry and live happily ever afterward. I'm absolutely nothing without you. . . . You're a necessity and a luxury and a darling, precious lover—and you're going to be a husband to your wife. . . ."*

Scott Fitzgerald knew he would be a husband, and there was every indication that he would be a world-famous author. On March 30 he sent a telegram to Zelda: WE WILL BE AW-FULLY NERVOUS UNTIL IT IS OVER. . . . FIRST EDITION OF THE BOOK IS SOLD OUT.

When Zelda Sayre got off the train in New York, she was radiant and beautiful, the perfect Southern belle, the fairy-tale princess who would marry her handsome prince. The wedding took place on a sunny day, April 3, in the rectory of St. Patrick's Cathedral. Mr. and Mrs. F. Scott Fitzgerald left the church confident that they would conquer the world.

CHAPTER FOUR

THIS SIDE OF PARADISE COULD ONLY HAVE BEEN WRITTEN by a young author. It is in many ways autobiographical, as are many first novels, and the author himself wrote, in response to a request for biographical material, to the Booksellers' Convention: *"I don't want to talk about myself because I'll admit I did that somewhat in this book. In fact to write it, it took three months; to conceive it—three minutes; to collect the data in it—all my life."*

It is the story of Amory Blaine, his college experiences, his life in the army, his settling in New York after the war and working for an advertising company, his romantic love affairs, and his monumental three-week drunken spree. It traces the evolution of an egotist into a "personage." Fitzgerald used excerpts from letters, poetry, and even dramatic dialogue in this hectic and often disorganized work. Eighteen years after its publication, he was probably right in his judgment that his first novel was "utterly spurious," and, to a new generation, "a pretty remote business." Nonetheless, he did record accurately what he saw and felt, and he captured with sensitivity the spirit of the times and of the generation he described as *"grown up to find all Gods dead, all wars fought, all faith in man shaken."*

Whatever the faults of *This Side of Paradise* appear to be now, it was a great success with the critics and the public in 1920. H. L. Mencken, America's most esteemed critic at the time, called it *"the best American novel I have seen of late . . . a truly amazing first novel—original in structure, extremely sophisticated in manner. . . ."* The reviewer for *The New York Times* wrote: *"The glorious spirit of abounding youth glows throughout this fascinating tale."* Harry Hansen, the important reviewer for the *Chicago Daily News*, called it *"probably one of the few really American novels extant."*

Throughout the country, the book was highly praised, though there were two notable dissenting opinions. In spite of some virtues, Edmund Wilson, whose continuing friendship with Fitzgerald never interfered with his objective literary judgments, thought the book was *"very immaturely imagined: it is always just verging on the ludicrous . . . one of the most illiterate books of any merit ever published. . . . It is not only full of bogus ideas and faked literary references but it is full of English words misused with the most reckless abandon."* Fitzgerald's college friend hit upon one of his weak points—his spelling was atrocious, and he even misspelled the name of Father Fay, to whom he dedicated the novel.

Fitzgerald took Wilson's criticism well, but one reaction

to the book disturbed him sufficiently to make him write a lengthy letter in reply. It came from John Grier Hibben, the president of Princeton, and it complained that the author had portrayed his university as a snobbish country club. Fitzgerald wrote:

"It was a book written with the bitterness of my discovery that I had spent several years trying to fit in with a curriculum that is after all made for the average student. After the curriculum had tied me up, taken away the honors I'd wanted, bent my nose over a chemistry book and said, 'No fun, no activities, no offices, no Triangle trips—no, not even a diploma if you can't do chemistry'—after that I retired."

He admitted that he had overaccentuated the university's country club atmosphere, but even in the midst of his literary and personal triumph, he could not forget the hurt that Princeton had inflicted on him.

This Side of Paradise was considered daring and alarmingly frank at the time of its publication. It was a best seller, and it made its twenty-three-year-old author a famous and sought-after man. For the older generation, it explained the behavior of their children; for the children, it justified a way of life that shocked their parents. The world was changing, and Scott Fitzgerald had recorded that change. *"America,"* he wrote later, *"was going on the greatest gaudiest spree in*

history and there was going to be plenty to tell about it."
He was a perceptive and sensitive observer, with an immense
gift for re-creating in words the atmosphere of the period,
for recording the speech and attitudes of his time. Physically
and emotionally, too, he and Zelda personified the epoch.
He was elegantly dressed and charming and witty; his new
bride, who had changed her wardrobe from Southern frills
to New York sophistication, was beautiful and wild and
fearless. They were ideally qualified to shock and amuse and
entertain, and more than willing to do so.

America had come through the austerity and idealism of
war and was tired of it. Life was, above all, to be enjoyed.
Every group was in rebellion—the workers demanded their
rights, women demanded their rights, and the young asked
to be heard in their revolt against the old American order
and morality. It was a time of defiance, during which young
women, who were called "flappers," wore thin dresses that
rose high above the ground, as well as having short sleeves;
they put on as much makeup as they pleased and they
smoked and drank with men. The moan of the saxophone
replaced the gentle hum of the violin in the ballroom, and
men and women danced daringly close together. Couples
went to dark rooms and to cars—another new liberating
force—to neck and to pet! Freud wrote about the importance of sex, and prohibition—making the drinking of alcohol illegal—only increased the consumption of alcohol.
Radio was born and broadened the horizons of all, and words

like *damn* and *hell* were heard on the stage. It was named the Jazz Age by F. Scott Fitzgerald, and who could better represent the unleashing of the new era than Fitzgerald himself and his dazzling young wife?

For a while, the Fitzgeralds acted their roles with joy and abandon; they wanted to shock and to call attention to themselves. They did handstands in the lobbies of fashionable hotels. They went to the theatre and horrified both audience and cast by laughing at the serious parts and remaining silent at the jokes. They hired taxis, and one of them sat on the roof while the other rode on the hood. The two of them spun around in a revolving door for half an hour. One evening Zelda dived into the fountain at Union Square fully dressed, and another evening her husband did a near-striptease in a Broadway theatre. They were out to have a good time, to defy every rule. Fitzgerald was delighted with his role and with all the money which was suddenly his.

Nonetheless, he was too sensitive to take it all seriously; in addition, it was a far too expensive and exhausting game. With his marvelous ability to analyze himself as well as others, Fitzgerald wrote:

"For just a moment before it was demonstrated that I was unable to play the role, I, who knew less of New York than any reporter of six months standing and less of its society than any hall-room boy in a Ritz stag line, was pushed into the position not only of spokesman of the time but of the

typical product of that same moment. I, or rather it was 'we' now, did not know exactly what New York expected of us and found it rather confusing. Within a few months after our embarkation on the Metropolitan venture we scarcely knew any more who we were and we hadn't a notion what we were. A dive into a civic fountain, a casual brush with the law, was enough to get us into the gossip columns, and we were quoted on a variety of subjects we knew nothing about."

The Fitzgeralds were, in spite of appearances, lost and lonely. After two months, they decided to leave the city, fleeing from the publicity that had made them play parts they thought they wanted to play but could not really play with ease. The town they chose to settle in for a while was Westport, Connecticut, a small town on Long Island Sound, not too far from Manhattan. At first they enjoyed the quiet outdoor life, but after a while it became oppressive; they found that they missed the people and the parties. Because of this, they went more and more frequently on visits to New York, and their Westport home became the scene of large and noisy weekend parties. The rhythm of their lives was no less exhausting than it had been in the city, but Fitzgerald did not forget his work and during the summer he started a novel called *The Flight of the Rocket*. He was optimistic and wrote Perkins that he expected to finish it by November first.

While her husband wrote, Zelda was becoming bored.

She did not enjoy the role of housekeeper and had no regard for the money that she spent as she pleased. Both of them drank too much; the result was a series of ugly quarrels, in spite of their love for each other. They wanted peace but seemed unable to enjoy it. Their financial situation, too, put a strain on Fitzgerald. His novel was selling well, and his income was a good one, but they managed to spend far more than he earned. This led to his need to borrow—from his publisher and from his agent. The money was always given to him as advance payment against future earnings, so he was under a constant, unnatural pressure to turn out more stories than he wanted to, more than he felt he could successfully create. For this reason, he could not have been surprised by the adverse critical response to a collection of his stories, *Flappers and Philosophers,* that Scribner's published in August. The same reviewers who had praised his novel turned against him. They accused him of being too slick and too commercial, not nearly up to the level of his highly praised novel.

By autumn it was clear that "country living" was not the solution to the Fitzgeralds' problems. They wanted the excitement of New York and they moved to a small apartment near the fashionable Plaza Hotel. Life was much as it had been before, with Fitzgerald alternating between a series of wild parties and stretches of hard work. The latter went well and at the end of the year he was able to write to his aunt and uncle:

"I am just putting the finishing touches on my novel. . . . It is much more carefully written than the first one and I have a good deal of faith in it tho it's so bitter and pessimistic that I doubt it'll have the popular success of the first. Still, as you know, I am in this game seriously and for something besides money. . . . I'd rather live on less and preserve the one duty of a sincere writer—to set down life as he sees it as gracefully as he knows how."

With this in mind, Fitzgerald finished his novel. He was fortunate, too, and did not have to live on less, since the prebook publication rights were sold to a magazine for seven thousand dollars, which enabled him to take Zelda away from New York to spend a summer in Europe. The trip would be shorter than planned, for Zelda was pregnant and they wanted the baby to be born in America.

Europe was a disappointment. They first spent a short time in England where they dined with the great popular novelist John Galsworthy, whom Fitzgerald liked but found to be too pessimistic. They then went to France, which they found a "bore and a disappointment." Finally, they went to Italy, which they liked even less. At the end of their trip they returned to London in time for the British publication of *This Side of Paradise,* but the reviews were so bad that they suddenly and enthusiastically decided to return home.

Upon their return to America, they had to decide where they wanted to live, the major consideration being where they wanted their child to be born. New York was out—"*It seemed inappropriate to bring a baby into all that glamour and loneliness*," Fitzgerald wrote. So at first they tried Montgomery, but they finally settled on St. Paul, where they rented a house.

He was a hero in St. Paul, the hometown boy who had made good in the big city, but Fitzgerald did not feel heroic. He had done little work for months and because of this felt restless and depressed. He wrote Perkins:

"*My 3rd novel, if I ever write another, will I am sure be black as death with gloom. I should like to sit down with ½ a dozen chosen companions and drink myself to death but I am sick alike of life, liquor and literature. If it wasn't for Zelda I think I'd disappear out of sight for three years. Ship as a sailor or something and get hard—I'm sick of the flabby semi-intellectual softness in which I flounder with my generation.*"

Fitzgerald knew only two ways to combat depression— alcohol, which paradoxically only increased his gloom, and hard work. In St. Paul, he chose the latter, renting a room in town in which to write. He put all his energies into his work; he read and revised the proofs of his novel, which was to be called *The Beautiful and Damned;* he wrote one of his best stories, "The Diamond as Big as the Ritz," and he worked on the first draft of a play. Zelda seemed relaxed and happy awaiting the birth of their child and helping her husband with his work, which he always showed to her for approval.

On October 26, the child was born and given the name Frances Scott. Fitzgerald sent a telegram to Zelda's parents that read: LILLIAN GISH IS IN MOURNING CONSTANCE TAL-MADGE IS A BACK NUMBER A SECOND MARY PICKFORD HAS ARRIVED.

The baby girl was beautiful and a source of joy, but Zelda soon began to feel trapped: caring for the child tied her down. Winter came and with it icy weather she had never before experienced. Besides, social life in St. Paul was limited. Fitzgerald, too, became nervous as the publication of his second novel approached. Once again, he worried over every detail, giving the publisher advice on the jacket design, the publicity, and the advertising. Therefore, they were both more than pleased to be able to go to New York in connection with the publication of *The Beautiful and Damned* on March 3.

The New York visit was not successful; both Fitzgeralds were drunk most of the few weeks they spent there. However, the novel was successfully launched. It is the story of Gloria and Anthony Patch, a glamorous, young, liberated couple who live a pleasure-seeking existence according to the fashion of the times. They end up desperate and degraded, victims of their own way of living. It is not a very good novel: it is too consciously literary, too confused, and the hero and heroine do not come to life. If *This Side of Paradise* was the spontaneous outcry of a young writer, *The Beautiful and Damned* is the effort of that young writer to carefully and artfully construct a "work of art."

However, Fitzgerald was fortunate that the critics, while voicing general disappointment in the novel, continued to speak of the author's great talent. The public, too, responded well. Fitzgerald was well known, his novel was supposed to be scandalous, and *The Beautiful and Damned* sold forty-three thousand copies.

Upon their return to St. Paul, Fitzgerald got back to work. He had to put together a second collection of stories that Scribner's would publish in the fall. To spare Zelda the problems of housekeeping, the couple spent their summer at a private yacht club, with the baby, whom they called Scottie, and a nurse. During this time, too, Fitzgerald had another idea for a novel on which he wanted to work, but he was haunted by financial pressures that might prevent him from completing his novel and thus spent his time turning out more commercially rewarding stories. No matter how much money he earned, he seemed forever to be in debt.

In the fall, they decided to return to New York; they had exhausted all of St. Paul's possibilities and Zelda dreaded the idea of another cold winter there. This time, however, New York would be different for them. They had done the things they had set out to do in the big city, they had had their fun—now they would be serious. New York no longer amused them as it once had; and the pressures on them would be lessened since, though they were still written about, they were no longer big news.

With this resolve in mind, they settled at the Plaza while looking for a home in the suburbs. For a while, their conscious effort paid off: there were no parties, and there was no alcohol. When they found a house that suited them in Great Neck on Long Island, they were happy to be leaving the city for the tranquillity of the country.

Great Neck, however, was hardly the place for the peaceful life that the Fitzgeralds had envisioned. Only thirty minutes from Broadway, it was or had been the home of many of the biggest names in the theatre: Lillian Russell, Eddie Cantor, George M. Cohan, Fannie Brice, and Florenz Ziegfeld. It was the setting for spectacular parties in spectacular homes, such as those given by Sam Buck, a musical comedy writer and assistant to Ziegfeld who lavishly entertained in his palatial home with its all-black dining room and orange study, which had been designed by a designer for the *Ziegfeld Follies*.

The Fitzgerald house was more modest, but the temptations of the extravagant Great Neck community were too strong for Scott and Zelda. They bought themselves a second-hand Rolls-Royce, hired a nurse to care for Scottie and a couple to run the house, and settled in. Settling in meant joining the parties at which they were most welcome guests, as well as giving wild and long ones of their own. If they

F. Scott Fitzgerald with Zelda and their daughter, Scottie.

Ring Lardner with his family.

didn't go to New York, New York came to them, and their house overflowed with people and chaos. The weekend parties were nonstop affairs, and semihumorous house rules had to be posted for the guests. Among them were: "Visitors are requested not to break down doors in search of liquor, even when authorized to do so by the host and hostess. Weekend guests are respectfully notified that invitations to stay over Monday, issued by the host and hostess during the small hours of Sunday morning, must not be taken seriously."

Life in Great Neck clearly did not offer Fitzgerald the peace he sought, but it did have certain advantages. It provided him with the background for one of his finest books, and it gave him an opportunity to meet a man who was to become one of his most treasured friends. The man was Ring Lardner, a successful sportswriter, a bitter satirist of the American scene. Eleven years older than Fitzgerald, Lardner too had come from the Midwest. His world—that of sports and entertainment—was different from that of Fitzgerald, but the two men found much in common and would spend long hours together, sometimes drinking throughout the night. Lardner was a brilliant and witty man, but he was also profoundly cynical. He showed a tragic penchant for self-destruction, which Fitzgerald understood all too well. He was, above all, deeply impressed with Lardner's wisdom, honesty, and extraordinary kindness. He encouraged and helped Lardner prepare his works for book publication, and the two men were inseparable the year and a half they were neighbors in Great Neck.

In spite of the frantic nature of the social life in Great Neck, Fitzgerald still managed to arrange periods of seclusion during which he worked on his novel. His stories were not going well—he felt they had lost their freshness and immediacy. Even the reviewers were disappointed in his latest collection, *Tales of the Jazz Age*, in spite of the fact that it included "The Diamond as Big as the Ritz" as well as another of his finest tales, "May Day."

However, writing the novel would take a long time, and Fitzgerald's hopes for the immediate future lay in his play,

The Vegetable, on which he had been working intermittently. In spite of praise from Edmund Wilson, who had been most enthusiastic about the manuscript, Fitzgerald had great difficulty finding a Broadway producer. When he finally did, his hopes were high—he had no doubt that the play would make him rich. Though compared to other writers he was already rich, his financial problems were worse than ever: in their first year in Great Neck, the Fitzgeralds had spent thirty-six thousand dollars. He was a successful, wealthy writer, yet he had no money. Things were so desperate that, a few weeks before his play opened, he was forced to write a pleading letter to Perkins, saying that *"If I don't in some way get $650.00 in the bank by Wednesday morning I'll have to pawn the furniture."*

The more he watched the rehearsals of his play, the more certain he was that its great success would save him. *The Vegetable* opened in Atlantic City on November 20, 1923, prior to Broadway. It told the story of a railroad clerk who is talked into running for President of the United States and in the end becomes the postman he has wanted to be all along.

It was a comic political satire, but the audience didn't laugh. Instead, they began to walk out en masse during the second act. Fitzgerald was crushed; he worked on revisions for a week, but nothing could save his play. *The Vegetable* never reached Broadway.

With the failure of his play, Fitzgerald realized that he

could be saved only by energetically working on more short stories. Once again, he showed that he did indeed have the strength to recover from defeat. Taking refuge in a bare room over his garage, he worked twelve hours a day for five weeks, after which he gradually relaxed this exhausting pace, but continued to work steadily and hard for several months. Only in this way could he make enough money to pay his debts and get sufficiently ahead to be able to devote full time to his novel.

As he reached this goal, he found it increasingly difficult to resist parties and even more difficult to resist drinking. There was always the feeling that alcohol might help him through difficult periods, though he knew it paralyzed his work. Now, having gone through a long period of pushing himself mercilessly, he began to drink again. But Scott Fitzgerald's antics under the influence of alcohol were no longer entertaining; instead, they became destructive. He would disappear for two or three days after which he would return home, sprawl out on his front lawn in the early hours of the morning and fall asleep. At parties, he was irritating rather than amusing. No one enjoyed watching him crawl under a dinner table or try to eat his soup with a fork. In his efforts to gain attention and in his fight against dullness, he himself was becoming dull.

The Fitzgeralds realized it was time for a change, and they decided they would find that change in Europe. They would live cheaply there and would not return to America until Scott had a solid accomplishment behind him. Zelda was not difficult to convince; she never wanted to stay in one place too long—"I hate a room without a suitcase in it," she said. "It seems so permanent."

Shortly before leaving for Europe, Scott Fitzgerald summed up his feelings in a letter to Maxwell Perkins:

"It is only in the last four months that I've realized how much I've, well, almost <u>deteriorated</u> in the three years since I finished The Beautiful and Damned. *The last four months of course I've worked but in the two years—over two years —before that, I produced exactly <u>one</u> play, <u>half a dozen</u> short stories and three or four articles—an average of about <u>one hundred</u> words a day. If I'd spent this time reading or traveling or doing anything—even staying healthy—it'd be different, but I spent it uselessly, neither in study nor in contemplation but only in drinking and raising hell generally. . . ."*

CHAPTER FIVE

PARIS WAS THE CENTER OF THE ARTISTIC WORLD WHEN Scott and Zelda Fitzgerald arrived there in 1924. The French capital drew to it artists, writers, and musicians from all over the world. Living there at the time of the Fitzgeralds' arrival were three of the literary masters of this century—James Joyce, Ezra Pound, and Gertrude Stein.

However, the Fitzgeralds were anxious to go toward the sunshine and stayed in Paris only a short time. While there, they met an extraordinary couple who were to play an important role in their lives: Sara and Gerald Murphy. In Gerald Murphy, Fitzgerald found a hero, a man to emulate. He was handsome, charming, and very rich. He knew good food and good wine and recognized good music and good art. Everyone who came into contact with Gerald Murphy delighted in his urbane company. He was, in many ways, the man Scott Fitzgerald wanted to be. His wife Sara was equally appealing—beautiful, intelligent, warm, and generous. The Murphys' money came from private incomes, and they knew how to spend it. Unlike most Americans who started to come to France in droves in the 1920s, they were not eccentric bohemians, but a family—with three children —who had simply decided that life would be more pleasant and livable in France than it was in the United States. Gerald Murphy painted and, through his work and taste, he had become a friend of the most important younger painters working in Paris—Picasso, Miró, Juan Gris, and Braque. The Murphys were equally at home in the worlds of music and dance and were on close terms with the great composer Stravinsky and the Russian impresario Diaghilev. They lived graceful, beautiful lives, and the Fitzgeralds were enchanted with them. The Murphys, too, found the Fitzgeralds most agreeable company—fresh and lively and intelligent, if somewhat misguided. And they told them of their discovery of the pleasures of the south of France, then a fairly unknown vacation area. The Murphys were building a home at the then-unspoiled coastal town of Antibes, and they arranged to meet the Fitzgeralds there in the summer.

Scott and Zelda left Paris for the south and within a short time found a sumptuous villa facing the Mediterranean outside the town of St. Raphaël. The landscape was luxuriant, the sea a deep, clear blue, and the climate gentle—it was the ideal place for Scott to work on his novel, undisturbed. For Zelda, there was swimming and sunning on the as yet unspoiled beaches. She did all she could to stay out of her husband's way so that he might concentrate on his work, but she was used to more activity and became restless. Fortunately, she made friends with a number of French aviators who frequented the same beach and who were charmed by her freshness and beauty.

Fitzgerald worked hard, happy that Zelda was distracted by the company of her new friends. Concerned only with his work, he was totally unaware that their marriage was on the brink of a serious crisis; for Zelda and one of the French flyers, Edouard Jozan, had fallen in love. Everyone but Fitzgerald, selfishly preoccupied, was aware of it. Jozan was daring and romantic and handsome; he was a physical creature, his temperament the opposite of Fitzgerald's moody intellectualism, and Zelda was fascinated. He paid attention to her in a way Scott was unable to.

When Fitzgerald found out, he was shattered. Infidelity did not fit into his pattern of romantic love. He thought he had given everything he had to Zelda—not realizing that he had perhaps been too self-absorbed—and could not understand how she could give even a part of herself to someone else. There was a violent showdown, after which Jozan disappeared from their lives. However, the damage was done and from Scott's point of view the marriage could never be the same. Unlike the heroes and heroines of his books, he could not tolerate the idea of a casual affair, of sexual promiscuity.

Shaken as he was by this episode, his drive and ego were such that nothing could interfere with his novel. In August he had confidently written to Perkins that his book was about the best American novel ever written. He also mentioned rather casually that he had been unhappy but that his work had not suffered from it. Zelda, on the other hand, was more deeply hurt by the aftereffects of her affair. She became depressed and made an ineffectual attempt at suicide. She had no novel to fall back on, and she saw that the marriage was endangered.

Scott was too preoccupied with his novel to think about his marriage. He worked so steadily that by the end of October, the manuscript of *The Great Gatsby* was sent to his publisher. Perkins's response was just what he wanted and needed; the editor agreed that it was Fitzgerald's finest work and was optimistic over its possibilities.

With his work on the novel behind him, Scott felt ready for a change. He was nearing a state of exhaustion after the intensive work of the past few months, and the couple were worn out from the emotional difficulties of their once-ideal marriage. They traveled through Italy, which they still didn't like, but Scott's mind was only on the forthcoming publication of his novel. In February he wrote to a critic and author, Ernest Boyd:

"My new novel appears in late March: The Great Gatsby. *It represents about a year's work and I think it's about ten years better than anything I've done. All my harsh smartness has been kept ruthlessly out of it—it's the greatest weakness*

(On the right) *Manuscript page from* The Great Gatsby.

In my younger and more vulnerable years my father told me something
that I've been turning over in my my mind ever since.

"When you feel like criticizing anyone," he said, "just
remember that everyone in this world hasn't had the
advantages that you've had."

He didn't say anymore but we've always been unusually
communicative in a reserved way and I understood that he
meant a great deal more than that. In consequence
I'm inclined to reserve all judgements, a habit that has opened
up many curious natures to me and also made me the victim
of not a few collossal bores. The abnormal mind is quick to
detect and attach itself to this quality when it appears in
a normal person, and so it came about that in
college I was unjustly accused of being a politician,
because I was privy to the secret griefs of wild, unknown
men. Most of the confidences were unsought — frequently
I have feigned sleep, preoccupation or a hostile levity
when I realized by some unmistakeable sign that an
intimate revelation was quivering on the horizon — for
the intimate revelations of young men or at any rate the
terms in which they express them vary no more than the heavenly
messages which reach us over the psychic radio.
Reserving judgements is a matter of infinite hope. I am still a little
afraid of missing something if I forget that, as my father snobbishly
suggested and I snobbishly repeat, a sense of the fundamental decencies
is parcelled out unequally at birth.

And after boasting this way of my tolerance, I come to the
admission that it has a limit. Conduct may be founded on the
hard rock or the wet marshes but after a certain point I
don't care what its founded on. When I came back here from the east
last autumn I felt that I wanted the world to be in uniform
and at a sort of moral attention forever; I wanted no more
riotous excursions with privileged glimpses into the human
heart. It was only Gatsby himself that was exempted from my

in my work, distracting and disfiguring it even when it calls up an isolated sardonic laugh. I don't think this has a touch left . . ."

The Fitzgeralds timed the end of their stay in Italy so that they might be back in Paris when *The Great Gatsby* was published in America. It would be easier to get word of the book's reception that way. Scott was almost euphoric on the trip back to France and wrote to John Peale Bishop:

"The cheerfulist things in my life are first Zelda and second the hope that my book has something extraordinary about it. I want to be extravagantly admired again. Zelda and I sometimes indulge in terrible four-days rows that always start with a drinking party, but we're still enormously in love and about the only truly happily married couple I know."

This was the romantic and unrealistic Fitzgerald writing of his marriage, without truly understanding Zelda's needs. However, his estimation of his novel was at least partially confirmed when two writers he respected highly, Gertrude Stein and T. S. Eliot, wrote him letters of extravagant praise. *"You are creating the contemporary world much as Thackeray did his,"* wrote Miss Stein. And Eliot said that the novel *"has interested and excited me more than any new novel I have seen, either English or American, for a number of years."* There were enthusiastic letters, too, from Edith

Wharton and Willa Cather as well as H. L. Mencken and Edmund Wilson. The newspaper reviews, though generally good, were not as perceptive as Fitzgerald would have wanted. *"I think all the reviews I've seen,"* he wrote to Perkins, *"except two, have been absolutely stupid and lousy. Someday they'll eat grass, by God! This thing, both the effort and the result, have hardened me and I think now I'm much better than any of the young Americans without exception."*

Fitzgerald's judgment has proven to be correct, and today *The Great Gatsby* is considered a classic. Its popularity has steadily increased throughout the years. A brilliantly conceived and executed novel, it achieves a rare artistic perfection. No summary can do justice to this deeply moving story of Jay Gatsby, a man who built his life upon a dream that turned out to be false. In telling Gatsby's story through the eyes of a sympathetic and believable narrator, against the background of a town similar to Great Neck, with its distorted values, Scott Fitzgerald created a masterpiece. He was not drawing on incidents or anecdotes from his own life, but from a perception of life itself.

The public, however, did not quickly appreciate the book's worth, and in Marseille, on his way to Paris, Fitzgerald had discouraging news. Perkins cabled him that sales of *Gatsby* were "doubtful." The book that he felt sure would bring him not only the recognition he deserved but also the money he needed was obviously not the success he had hoped for. Bitterly, he wrote Perkins:

"In all events I have a book of good stories for the fall. Now I shall write some cheap ones until I've accumulated enough for my next novel. When that is finished and published I'll wait and see. If it will support me with no more intervals of trash I'll go on as a novelist. If not, I'm going to quit, come home, go to Hollywood and learn the movie business. I can't reduce this scale of living and I can't stand this financial insecurity."

Fitzgerald had put his heart as well as his enormous talent into *The Great Gatsby*, yet even that didn't seem enough. He and others found possible reasons for the novel's failure with the public: it wasn't long enough, it had no important female character. But the fact remained that a major novel was not recognized as such by the public at the time of its publication.

Fitzgerald had every reason to feel hurt and depressed when he and Zelda returned to Paris. They rented an apartment in the center of the city and saw that Scottie was looked after by a nurse. Then they embarked on a period characterized by Fitzgerald as one of "1000 parties and no work."

However, even when not working well, he was passionately interested in literature. Six months before, Fitzgerald had written to Perkins to recommend to him the work of a young American writer named Ernest Hemingway, and one of the first things he did upon his return to the French capital in the winter of 1925 was to meet Hemingway. Their

Ernest Hemingway in front of Shakespeare and Company.

first encounter was at a bar. The rugged, athletic Hemingway was embarrassed by Fitzgerald's praise and taken aback by his drinking habits—by the end of their first meeting, Fitzgerald was almost in a stupor. However, the two men soon became close friends. Fitzgerald took a great and unselfish interest in the younger writer's work, arranged to have Scribner's publish a collection of his stories, and later gave him valuable editorial advice on his novel *The Sun*

Sara and Gerald Murphy on the beach at Antibes.

Also Rises. Hemingway was, in a way, a "competitor," but Fitzgerald never failed to help him in any way possible. Their relationship was a confused one, compounded of jealousy and misunderstanding as well as mutual respect, but Fitzgerald always admired and paid attention to Ernest Hemingway. Nor did he ever fail to help any writer whom he believed deserving.

Nonetheless, his own career was going badly, and in August, when all the French went on holiday, the Fitzgeralds followed the crowds to Antibes, which the Murphys had already made fashionable for the international set. Fitzgerald's letter to John Peale Bishop shows that, in spite of his despair, he had not lost his capacity for ironically summarizing a situation: *"There was no one at Antibes this summer except me, Zelda, the Valentinos, the Murphys, Mistinguet, Rex Ingram, Dos Passos, Alice Terry, the MacLeishes, Charlie Brackett, Maude Kahn, Esther Murphy, Marguerite Namara, E. Phillips Oppenheim, Mannes the violinist, Floyd Dell, Max and Crystal Eastman, ex-Premier Orlando, Etienne de Beaumont—just a real place to rough it, an escape from the world."* By listing some of the best-known celebrities of the time, he made his point.

When the summer came to an end, they returned to Paris where Fitzgerald planned to work on his new novel; but he found it impossible to make any real progress. Frustrated, his need to drink became more acute than ever. Paris was exciting and alive as few cities have ever been, but Scott and

Zelda, whose drinking had also reached a dangerous level, were too blinded by alcohol to see or feel it. They both lost touch with reality, and their antics while drunk seemed pathetic. Once the most welcome guests at any party, they were becoming a nuisance and an embarrassment. Their charm was gone and what remained was an unpleasant ability to offend.

Fortunately, they found support in the Murphys, who remained sympathetic though genuinely worried by the Fitzgeralds' penchant for self-destruction. However, there were few friends as protective and understanding as the Murphys. The others were merely repulsed and disenchanted.

Fitzgerald, in his sober moments, kept working on the novel, but to no avail. In the past, he had been able to alternate those crippling periods of drinking with periods of intensive work, but that no longer seemed to be the case. Even worse, in spite of his frantic attempts to do so, he was not enjoying life. He was unhappy in France and planned to return to America as soon as his novel was completed. *"You remember,"* he wrote to Perkins, *"I used to say I wanted to die at thirty—well, I'm now twenty-nine and the prospect is still welcome. . . ."* Nothing was working out the way he had planned.

Paradoxically, and temporarily, things began to go well for Fitzgerald during the first few months of 1926—though they were not a result of his present activity. A dramatic version of *The Great Gatsby*, adapted for the stage by Owen Davis, was having a successful Broadway run, and this led to its being bought for the movies. In addition, his new collection of short stories, *All the Sad Young Men,* was published to great critical acclaim; those critics who had liked but failed to evaluate *Gatsby* properly now had their chance to proclaim Fitzgerald's talents. They particularly praised one story, "The Rich Boy." *All the Sad Young Men* sold very well for a collection of short stories, enabling the author to pay his debts—for the moment, at least.

Nonetheless, Fitzgerald was not writing and as a result he was deeply depressed, as he always was when not involved in his work. In fact, he wrote nothing publishable between February 1926 and June 1927. The years abroad had been largely wasted, and on December 26, 1926, Scott and Zelda Fitzgerald, she nervous and weary, and he almost broken spiritually, returned to the United States to begin again. Their lofty ambitions were perhaps forgotten—they returned to their country not as the fairy-tale prince and princess of old, but as a prematurely exhausted and weary young couple hoping to make sense of their lives.

As soon as they arrived in America, an offer came from Hollywood. A major studio wanted Fitzgerald to write a college story for its star Constance Talmadge. Here was the chance he had been waiting for. Suddenly filled with confidence—he was, after all, in the eyes of the world, a popular and important writer—he set out for Hollywood, thus making good the threat made to Maxwell Perkins just a year before.

Hollywood was bursting with excitement when Scott and

Zelda, Scottie, and F. Scott Fitzgerald.

Zelda Fitzgerald arrived. It was the beginning of sound pictures, and 1927 was the year of *The Jazz Singer,* starring Al Jolson, the first part-talking film. *Ben Hur,* a spectacular film the Fitzgeralds had watched being made in Rome, was breaking box-office records, and Cecil B. De Mille was having great success with his extravagant costume movie *The King of Kings.*

The Fitzgeralds were greeted enthusiastically, and they in turn were thrilled by the movie capital's wealth and opulence. They moved into a four-apartment bungalow at the fashionable Ambassador Hotel, their neighbors being the great stars John Barrymore and Carmel Myers, as well as the writer Carl Van Vechten. Amidst the glamorous stars of Hollywood, they too were treated as stars. They had been given another chance.

Once again, however, their pranks got out of hand. At a party given for them by Carmel Myers, at which they were to be presented to Hollywood's elite, they removed all the ladies' pocketbooks from the cloakroom and boiled them in tomato sauce. Few if any thought this or similar childish pranks amusing. It was not an auspicious start.

Nonetheless, the Fitzgeralds thoroughly enjoyed their stay in Hollywood, which was marred only by the studio's finally deciding against the production of *Lipstick,* the movie on which Fitzgerald was working. As a parting gesture to the movies, Scott and Zelda put all the hotel furniture in the middle of their room and topped it with a pile of all their unpaid bills.

Fitzgerald had failed in his first attempt as a screenwriter, and now it was again time for him to work on his novel. The temptations of social life were clearly too great for him to resist, so with the help of friends he found an enormous, stately old mansion at Ellerslie near Wilmington, Delaware, where he felt sure he would find the peace and quiet he needed to return to work. Scott and Zelda were determined and did all they could to organize a "normal" household. Family life centered around Scottie, a uniting force for her parents as well as a delightful child, and Zelda's parents as well as Scott's came to visit. He went to nearby Princeton to watch the football games and rediscovered his youthful enthusiasm for sports. As a part of this new and well-disciplined life, he went to work on the novel. However, no matter how much they tried, there was no way they could prevent the marriage from disintegrating—the spark which had once sustained them had gone out, and they were unprepared for serenity and order. They had a degree of privacy for the first time, and they didn't know what to do with it. They had never been without outside stimulation and apparently required it. They made an effort to cut down on their drinking and became a part of the regular social life of Wilmington, but in their moments alone together life became what Scott Fitzgerald called "an organized dog and cat fight."

While Scott had his work to sustain him, Zelda once again grew restless. She had wanted to write and had even written some published magazine articles, but her husband remained the famous author. For a while she turned to painting and finally to ballet. She needed something in which to channel her creative energies. Dancing—she had loved it as a child—became a serious matter and she went several times a week to Philadelphia to study. Perhaps this was the real means of expression for her, a way of asserting herself, though her age—almost twenty-eight—was against her, since a ballet dancer must begin to study in childhood.

Bored and belligerent by the summer of 1928, the Fitzgeralds used the excuse of Zelda's wanting to further her ballet studies to return to Paris. It was another unproductive and unhappy summer, one Fitzgerald accurately summed up in the ledger he kept. *"July—drinking and general unpleasantness; August—general aimlessness."*

There were bright moments, however, such as Fitzgerald's meeting with the great Irish writer James Joyce. Overwhelmed at being in the great man's presence, he could only express his profound respect by offering to throw himself out of the window in solemn tribute. Joyce was alarmed. "That young man must be mad," he commented. "I'm afraid he'll do himself injury." At another time, Fitzgerald drew a picture of Joyce sitting at a table wearing a halo, a humble Fitzgerald on his knees beside him.

He also came to know two of the leading American literary personalities in Paris at the time: Sylvia Beach, part owner of the adventurous expatriates' bookshop Shakespeare and

Company, and Janet Flanner, a sensitive journalist. Sylvia Beach and her partner Adrienne Monnier grew very fond of the young American writer—they were charmed by his blue eyes and good looks, "that wild recklessness of his and his fallen-angel fascination." Janet Flanner, too, found him delightful company, even when he woke her up at two in the morning to discuss literature.

These women were the exceptions; most of Fitzgerald's acquaintances in Paris were tired of him and of his wife. The couple drank constantly—in spite of Zelda's real dedication to her ballet studies—and they spent their money with reckless abandon.

By September, when it was time to return to Ellerslie, they were close to despair. In spite of the fact that he had made a great deal of money—almost thirty thousand dollars in 1927 and 1928—they were practically penniless. In addition, their quarrels, intensified by the effects of alcohol, were almost unbearably bitter. The romance had come to an end. They had married as a fairy-tale prince and princess and were apparently unprepared to deal with the realities of their situation.

The fall and winter in Delaware were no better. Zelda danced, with an unhealthy compulsive drive, frantically eager to show that she could be "someone." And Scott drank heavily, disappearing from his home night after night, all too often ending up in a local police station after a senseless, drunken brawl. He wrote optimistically to Perkins that his new novel was coming along well and that he would send him two chapters per month, but there was no reasonable hope of his keeping his promise.

Fitzgerald's marriage was collapsing and he was unable to work seriously; despair drove him to drink, and drink paralyzed his efforts to repair his marriage or go forward with his work.

All seemed hopeless when, in the spring of 1929, they gave up their home at Ellerslie and returned again to Europe. Their stay in Paris was characteristically unhappy. Zelda wrote: *"I worked constantly and was terribly superstitious and moody about my work . . . I lived in a quiet, ghostly, hyper-sensitized world of my own. Scott drank."*

The break between the couple seemed complete, and they were unable to go on pretending to the world that they were the ideally happy and joyous couple they had seemed. In the summer, they returned to the south of France, but it was no longer the pure, sparkling, flower-filled spot the Murphys had helped found. Instead it was cluttered with tourists and new buildings; and worst of all, no one was particularly interested in Scott and Zelda Fitzgerald.

Even the Murphys had lost their patience. Innately well-mannered, gentle people, they were offended by the Fitzgeralds' rudeness. When Scott and Zelda were not invited to a Murphy party, they retaliated by standing outside the garden wall and throwing garbage into the assembled group of guests. Scott had already caused considerable embarrassment at other Murphy parties. At one, he senselessly tossed ashtray after ashtray over the side of a table; at another he had thrown fruit at a distinguished lady guest, and at another he hurled wineglasses over the wall. These sophomoric attempts to attract attention disgusted the Murphys, and at one point Fitzgerald was banished from their home for three weeks.

During this period, Fitzgerald further infuriated the Murphys by telling them he had planned to use them as central characters in his novel, and spending hours openly observing and studying them. In addition, he kept asking them rude and unnecessarily intimate questions regarding their past and their life together. In the beginning, they were patient, but at a party one evening Sara Murphy felt she could take no more. She lashed out at Fitzgerald, reminding him that asking questions was no way to get to know people; that, in fact, he really knew nothing at all about human beings. *"Scott turned practically green,"* Gerald Murphy has recalled. *"He got up from the table and pointed his finger at her and said that nobody had ever dared say that to him . . ."*

During this period, Zelda was strangely removed and detached; she seemed to be in a world of her own, indifferent to her surroundings, interested only in her ballet studies. By the time the Fitzgeralds were ready to leave the south of France, Scott too seemed to have reached the end of his endurance. He wrote to Ernest Hemingway on September 9, 1929:

"My latest tendency is to collapse about 11:00 and, with the tears flowing from my eyes or the gin rising to their level and leaking over, tell interested friends or acquaintances that I haven't a friend in the world and likewise care for nobody, generally including Zelda, and often implying current company—after which the current company tend to become less current and I wake up in strange rooms in strange places. . . ."

The Paris winter was cold and depressing. Zelda was disheartened over her failure to make her mark as a professional dancer, and Scott, under the influence of gin, grew more and more offensive. In a desperate move to recapture their romance and regain their health, they went to Algiers in February.

When they returned to Paris, Zelda threw herself into her ballet classes with more vigor than ever—everything seemed to depend on her dancing; it was her whole life.

Early in April she gave a luncheon at her apartment. In the midst of the meal, one of her friends noticed that she was becoming tense. She said she was afraid she'd be late for her ballet lesson, and her friend offered to accompany her to the class. In the taxi on the way, Zelda started to shake; she suddenly began to change into her ballet costume while riding in the cab. She had no time to waste. When they were caught in a traffic jam, she jumped out of the taxi and ran frantically to the ballet studio.

It was the first concrete sign that she was seriously ill,

though friends had in the past noticed her peculiar behavior, had even suspected insanity. Within a few weeks, Zelda was hospitalized—it was the beginning of a long nightmare.

CHAPTER SIX

THE DOCTORS AT THE MENTAL HOSPITAL IN PRANGINS, Switzerland, diagnosed Zelda's illness as schizophrenia. She had withdrawn from the real world and was living in a troubled, turbulent state. They told her husband that there was one chance in four of total recovery, and two chances in four of partial recovery.

During the first few months she refused to see Scott, and when meetings were arranged she would break out in terrible attacks of eczema. Nonetheless, he stayed in Switzerland, to be by her side when she needed him. But he, too, was not in full control of himself. The doctors pleaded with him to stop drinking, explaining that his alcoholism haunted Zelda, but it was beyond his power to stop. In spite of the doctors' assurances that the illness had its origins in Zelda's childhood, he could not help feeling partially responsible.

During the time she was in Prangins, Zelda wrote stories, and when she was again able to see him, she showed them to Scott who liked them and tried to get Perkins to publish them, but his editor did not feel they were worthy of publication.

Except for occasional visits to Paris, where Scottie was attending school, and a trip to the States for his father's funeral and a visit to the Sayres to explain their daughter's illness, Fitzgerald spent most of his time in Switzerland. He drank heavily, miraculously being able to stop from time to time in order to write a short story which would enable him to pay some of his bills. He was a thoroughly professional writer when he had to be: during the fourteen months that Zelda was in the Swiss hospital, he wrote twelve short stories.

Zelda improved steadily, and in September 1931 she was well enough to leave the hospital and return to America. The couple decided to settle in Montgomery, where she would be near her family and he could quietly work on his novel.

Her family and friends were shocked by Zelda's appearance. No longer the vitally beautiful young woman, she was wan and haggard. Scott, however, was confident that she would fully recover; there was a new and better feeling between them and they believed for a while that, with Scott understanding Zelda's needs, there might be a brighter outlook for the future.

Shortly after their return to Montgomery, Fitzgerald was given a second chance at Hollywood. He would be paid twelve hundred dollars a week to write a script based on a novel called *Red-Headed Woman*. When he arrived in the movie capital, he was not the confident young man who had been there four years before. He was nervous, and his nervousness caused him to drink too much again. Several years later he summed up this second Hollywood experience in a letter to Scottie:

"I ran afoul of a bastard named de Sano, since a suicide, and let myself be gypped out of command. I wrote the picture and he changed as I wrote . . . Result—a bad script. I left with the money, for this was a contract for weekly payments, but disillusioned and disgusted, vowing never to go back, tho they said it wasn't my fault and wanted me to stay. I wanted to get East when the contract expired to see how your mother was. . . ."

Zelda was, tragically, ill again. Her father had died and with him a solid, disciplined part of her life. She took his death badly, suffered a severe asthma attack, and became hysterical. Fitzgerald was horrified and frightened. His hopes for a normal life had been raised, but now there was nothing to do but send Zelda back to the hospital.

Zelda entered the Phipps Psychiatric Clinic in Baltimore on February 12, 1932, and Scott stayed behind in Montgomery to take care of Scottie. He had to write, too, in order to pay the mounting school and hospital bills, and during the first five months of 1932 he turned out four short stories. They were not his best work, but they would help him pay his debts.

While at Phipps, Zelda spent her time writing her first

novel and when it was completed she sent a copy of the manuscript directly to Maxwell Perkins, without first showing it to Scott. When he finally saw it, he was enraged. She had used specific incidents in their life, had borrowed material from his unfinished novel, and had portrayed him in an unfavorable light. He refused to allow it to be published unless the changes he demanded were made and Perkins gave in to his demands. His wife's defiance was a blow to Scott, and he never fully recovered from his anger at what he felt to be Zelda's betrayal of him. Nor did publication of the book, called *Save Me the Waltz,* help Zelda. It was badly received by the critics and sold poorly.

When it became clear in May of 1932 that Zelda would need a long period of treatment at Phipps, Fitzgerald and Scottie left Montgomery for Baltimore. Though Zelda would have to return to the hospital at regular intervals, she would be able to spend half of her time at home.

Fitzgerald found and rented a large rambling Victorian house which suited their needs. It was called "La Paix," which is French for "peace," but life there was anything but peaceful. The pressures on Scott were enormous; he was determined to work on his novel, he had to be both mother and father to his daughter, and he had to care for Zelda. The strain was too much for him, and he drank incessantly. He felt lonely and isolated in his battle to save his family, and he couldn't sleep. His physical health was failing, and the psychiatrists he visited in connection with Zelda's condition felt that he himself was in danger of an emotional collapse.

There were bitter and violent quarrels at home, too, during which wildly unreasonable accusations were exchanged. Zelda wrote and painted, and Scott, out of a sense of duty, often helped her with her writing. However, he resented her work: *he* was the writer in the family and must unequivocally be recognized as such.

At the same time, and in spite of his drinking, he worked on his novel. He was almost obsessed with it and would sit for hours at his desk, paying no attention to the smell of stale smoke and gin that filled the room. From time to time, he would get up and, in his old bathrobe, pace through the corridors of the enormous old house.

The novel was all he could cling to, with a disintegrating family life, huge expenses, and an income in 1932 that was half what he had earned the previous year. The novel and his small daughter were his consolations. The former could restore his reputation, while Scottie's charm and vitality buoyed his spirits.

However, the tension at home between him and Zelda, though never defined, continued throughout the following year and reached such a pitch that Fitzgerald even investigated the possibility of divorce. He was clearly as bad for Zelda as she was for him. Over and over again the doctors told him that matters might improve if he gave up drinking, but it was beyond his power.

He worked on the novel with fury: nothing would stop him. In the early summer, Zelda inadvertently started a fire by burning some clothes in a faulty fireplace. The house was badly in need of repairs, but Fitzgerald urged the landlord not to have the work done until he had completed his book. It was better for him to work amidst debris than be interrupted.

Late in the year, *Tender Is the Night* was finished, after which, in a rush of activity, Fitzgerald turned out five short stories for the *Post*. Not that he wanted to: he had to have the money and he still had the strength to work for it. In another move to get out of debt, they left La Paix and moved to a smaller house in Baltimore. At the same time, Zelda's condition worsened, and she was again hospitalized at the beginning of 1934. Any hope of her permanent recovery had vanished; Scott's only means of salvation was his novel, to which he had given a large part of his life.

Tender Is the Night was published in *Scribner's Magazine* in four installments from January through April 1934. Book publication was set for mid-April, and he was tense and nervous as the April date approached. He wondered if he was still gifted, if all his enormous efforts had been worthwhile. This was his most deeply felt book, his most personal, the one with which he identified most closely. Shortly before publication, he wrote to Perkins: *"I have lived so long*

(On the right) *A galley proof of* Tender Is the Night *with Fitzgerald's revisions.*

went into the room next to them and told a collapsed psychiatrist that he was better, always better, and the man tried to read his face for conviction, since he hung on the real world only through the reassurance he could find in the resonance, or lack of it, in Doctor Diver's voice. After that Dick discharged a shiftless orderly and it was time for luncheon. Meals with the patients were a chore he approached with apathy. The gathering, which of course did not include residents at the Eglantine or the Beeches, was conventional enough at first sight but over it brooded always a heavy melancholy. Such doctors as were present kept up a conversation but most of the patients, as if exhausted by their morning's endeavor, or depressed by the company, spoke little, and ate looking into their plates.

Luncheon over, Dick returned to his villa. Nicole was in the salon wearing a strange expression. He scented trouble and asked quickly: "What is it, dear?"

"Read that."

She tossed him a letter. It was from a woman recently discharged, though with skepticism on the part of the faculty. It accused him in no uncertain terms of having seduced her daughter who had been at her mother's side during the crucial stage of the illness. It presumed that Mrs. Diver would be glad to have this information and learn what her husband was really like.

Dick read the letter again. Couched in clear and concise English he yet recognized it as the letter of a manic. Upon a single occasion he had let the girl, a flirtatious little brunette, ride into Zurich with him upon her request, and in the evening had brought her back to the clinic. On the way back, in an idle, almost indulgent way, he kissed her. Later, she tried to carry the affair further but he was not interested and subsequently, perhaps consequently, the girl had come to dislike him, and taken her mother away before the proper time.

"This letter is deranged," he said casually. "I had no relations of any kind with that girl. I didn't even like her."

"Yes, I've tried thinking that," said Nicole.

"Surely you don't believe it?"

"I've been sitting here."

He sank his voice to a reproachful note and sat beside her. "This is absurd. This is a letter from a mental patient."

"I was a mental patient."

He stood up and spoke more authoritatively.

"We're not going to have any nonsense, Nicole. Go and round up the children and we'll start."

In the car, with Dick driving, they rounded the lake, following its little promontories, catching the burn of light and water in the windshield, tunnelling through cascades of evergreen. It was Dick's particular car, a Renault so dwarfish that they all stuck out of it except the children, between whom Mademoiselle towered mast-like in the rear seat. They knew every kilometer of the road—where they would smell the pine needles and the black stove smoke; a high sun with a face traced on it beat fierce on the straw hats of the children.

Nicole was silent; Dick could make nothing of her straight hard gaze. Often he felt lonely with her, and frequently she tired him with the flood of personal revelations she reserved exclusively for him, "I'm like this—I'm more like that," but this afternoon he would have liked her to rattle on in staccato for a while and give him glimpses of her thoughts. The situation held most threat of trouble when she backed up into herself and closed the doors behind her.

At Zug Mademoiselle got out and left them. In their well-burnished chariot the Divers approached the Agiri Fair through a menagerie of mammoth steam-rollers that made way for them, the drivers fixing the pleasure car reproachfully with Italian eyes. Dick parked the car, and as Nicole looked at him without moving, he said: "Come on, dear." Her lips drew apart into a sudden awful smile, and his belly quailed, but as if he hadn't seen it he repeated: "Come on. So the children can get out."

within the circle of this book and with these characters that often it seems to me that the real world does not exist but that only these characters exist . . . their glees and woes are just as important to me as what happens in life."

Because *Tender Is the Night* meant so much to him, Fitzgerald was deeply hurt by the book's lukewarm reception by both the critics and the public. He could not understand that, to both, the novel seemed old-fashioned, evoking an era that was no longer of interest. America was in the midst of social upheaval. Contemporary problems concerning the American way of life, the struggle of the underdog, and social justice were of greatest interest to readers who were for that reason buying the works of Sinclair Lewis and John Steinbeck. The problems of a wealthy couple on the French Riviera seemed remote and of little interest.

Nonetheless, the appeal of *Tender Is the Night* is universal and timeless. Drawing on Zelda's and his own tragic experience, even quoting verbatim from some of her letters to him, Fitzgerald told the story of Nicole, a beautiful and wealthy young woman afflicted with mental illness, who falls in love with her doctor, Dick Diver, while under treatment at a hospital in Switzerland. She marries him, and they live a life of glamour and excitement throughout Europe—largely in the south of France. Gradually, Nicole regains her health and in the process Dr. Diver falls apart. In the end, Nicole leaves him for another man, and Diver, by then an alcoholic, returns to America, destroyed.

For this novel, Fitzgerald obviously drew on his own experiences with Zelda. In the beginning of the book, when the pleasures of their gracious living are described, he bases his characters on Gerald and, to a lesser extent, Sara Murphy. Halfway through the novel, they become Scott and Zelda Fitzgerald. Life on the French coast is an accurate picture of the life they led in the twenties, and two of the lesser but very well-drawn characters, Abe North and Rosemary Hoyt, have their origins in Ring Lardner and Lois Moran, a Hollywood starlet who had been a good friend of Fitzgerald's. Fitzgerald was criticized for "borrowing" from the lives of his friends to enrich his novel, but the result was an enduring work of art.

It is not a perfectly constructed novel, as was *The Great Gatsby*, but it is an unforgettable and deeply moving one. Even Fitzgerald recognized certain structural flaws and worked on improving it at various intervals during his lifetime. Whatever its flaws, as Fitzgerald himself said to Gerald Murphy (whose wife was not at all pleased with the confusion of characters), "it has magic."

By the end of 1934, Scott Fitzgerald had to face two cruel facts: his career as a writer was going downhill, and all hopes of a normal marriage were gone. Writing was his sole means of expression and his profession, and he could not give that up. However, Zelda was pathetically beyond his help, and any major effort on his part to "cure" her would only destroy him. What he wrote a few years later applied to

Dick Diver as well as to himself: *"I think the pull of an afflicted person upon a normal one is at all times downward, depressing and eventually paralyzing, and it should best be left to those who have chosen such duties as a life work."*

The next two years were spent in a desperate attempt to understand himself and his failures, while trying to carry on a normal existence. His physical health—always weak—was deteriorating, and he frequently retreated to small towns in the South to find peace and recovery. Early in 1935, he traveled to Tryon, North Carolina, where he tried to cure himself of a liver disease, and later in the year he spent a long period of time in Asheville, North Carolina, to undergo treatment for tuberculosis. His "normal" life consisted of grinding out one publishable story after another, caring for Scottie, and trying to make a home for Zelda when the latter was well enough to visit.

The problems seemed insuperable, however. Scribner's published a collection of stories, *Taps at Reveille*, to follow his novel, and it sold poorly. His income was drastically reduced. To relieve the enormous financial burden, he could have sent Scottie to a public school and had Zelda committed to a public institution, but he couldn't bring himself to do either.

At the end of 1935, he fled, distraught, to the small town of Hendersonville, North Carolina. He had no more money, he was a broken man: somehow he had to find out what had happened to him and to his dreams. *"I only wanted absolute quiet to think out why I had developed a sad attitude toward* sadness, a melancholy attitude toward melancholy and a tragic attitude toward tragedy—why I had become identified with the objects of my horror or compassion."

In Hendersonville, he lived on cans of meat, a few oranges, a couple of cans of beer, and some crackers. His underwear consisted of a pair of pajama pants and a union suit. A few pairs of socks and two handkerchiefs completed his essential wardrobe.

While there, however, he thought, and he put his thoughts to writing: he began three articles that would eventually be published in *Esquire* magazine as "The Crack-Up." They are painfully personal and intimate pieces describing honestly his descent from the heights of success to the depths of failure, his sudden need to be alone, his realization that *"for two years of my life I had been drawing on resources I did not possess, that I had been mortgaging myself physically and spiritually up to the hilt . . ."* He described himself as a cracked plate and wondered if he was worth saving.

At the beginning of 1936, it might have seemed to many that Fitzgerald was not worth saving. He was in terrible physical condition and was frequently hospitalized. His stories were not selling, and there was every reason to believe he had lost his ability to write. The "Crack-Up" pieces were published and again drew attention to his talent as a writer, though they made him sound like a thoroughly defeated man. Hemingway, whom he continued to admire, was offended by their tone of surrender.

In April, he settled in Asheville, and Zelda was admitted

to a nearby sanitarium, Highland, where she would spend most of the rest of her life. Scott made a courageous effort to pull himself together, but in July disaster—inevitable, it seemed—struck again. In an attempt to show off his questionable athletic skills, he took a dive into the water from a fifteen-foot board and badly tore his shoulder muscles. This was followed by a bad fall in his bathroom, which resulted in a painful arthritis, and he was bedridden until the fall. He had nothing but time on his hands, and he began to brood on his impossible fate. He drank heavily and reached dangerous depths of depression. The more he considered his plight, the more he found it hopeless. He seemed to have no future, his income in 1936 had been only $10,180 and his debts four times that amount.

The pressure was only temporarily relieved in September, when his mother died, leaving him some money. His mother's death affected him more than he would have expected. For years he had resented her, while pitying his ineffectual father, and they had corresponded only occasionally, but her death made him feel sorrow at *"her prides and sorrows and disappointments all come to nothing."* He described the money he received from her as *"the luckiest event of some time. She was a defiant old woman, defiant in her love for me in spite of my neglect for her, and it would have been quite within her character to have died that I might live."*

A permanent solution to his financial worries had to be found, and for two years the thought of trying Hollywood

Fitzgerald in front of the Algonquin Hotel in New York in 1937.

again had been in the back of his mind. His books were going badly as were his magazine pieces. No one cared any more about F. Scott Fitzgerald. Only Hollywood could offer him the chance to make some money. He had asked Harold Ober to sound out the possibilities, and in June 1937 an offer was finally made. Ironically, Ober's Hollywood representative first turned down that offer as an "insult" to his client's ability, but Scott was approached personally and eagerly accepted. In his present state, that offer of a six-month contract at a thousand dollars a week was not an insult; it was a lifesaver.

This was his best chance to clear up his past debts and make a brilliant new career for himself. Always worried about debts and concerned with financial matters, he arranged to have his salary sent to Harold Ober. From this money Ober would pay Fitzgerald four hundred dollars to cover his own, Scottie's, and Zelda's expenses; the rest would go toward paying Fitzgerald's debts.

A new start in Hollywood would be his chance, his last chance.

CHAPTER SEVEN

Scott Fitzgerald felt he had a new lease on life when he left for Hollywood in July 1937. He would not only be a successful writer there, but a director as well. The future lay with the movies rather than with books. He had a concrete plan of action, avoiding the mistakes he had made on his first trips to the Coast, and on the train he wrote to Scottie: *"I must be very tactful but keep my hand on the wheel from the start—find out the key man among the bosses and the most malleable among the collaborators—then fight the rest tooth and nail until, in fact or in effect, I'm alone on the picture. That's the only way I can do my best work. Given a break I can make them double this contract in less than two years . . ."*

Though he felt refreshed and newly optimistic when he arrived in Hollywood, Fitzgerald's friends found him a changed man. To them he had lost his spirit and seemed frightened. His pale and wrinkled face reflected his years of turmoil.

After moving into the Garden of Allah Hotel—home of other writers, famed scriptwriters such as Marc Connelly,

Dorothy Parker, John O'Hara, and Robert Benchley—he began on a script for *A Yank at Oxford*. He worked seriously, making every effort to master a new technique, and though his contribution to the picture was not used, he felt he had learned a great deal in the process. The next script he was given to write was for a film called *Three Comrades*; he enjoyed his work on it and felt he had done a good job. He was reconciled to remaining in Hollywood and wrote to friends in the East:

"It is the kind of life I need. I think I'm through drinking for good now, but it's a help this first year to have the sense that you are under observation . . . it wouldn't help this budding young career to be identified with John Barleycorn. In free-lance writing it doesn't matter a damn what you do with your private life as long as your stuff is good; but I had gotten everything pleasant that drink can offer long ago and really do not miss it at all and rather think of that last year and a half in Baltimore and Carolina as a long nightmare. . . ."

Sadly, many people had forgotten who Scott Fitzgerald was, and others thought he was dead, but many others remembered his better days, and he was quickly invited to join in Hollywood's glamorous social life. He did so for a while, but it soon became apparent that his weak health would not permit him to do so. What he needed was a woman to care for him and for him to love; he corresponded regularly with Zelda and continued to assume responsibility for her, but he looked on her with a mixture of compassion and bitterness. Their marriage, in all but a legal sense, was over.

At a party at Robert Benchley's, he met the woman he needed. Her name was Sheilah Graham, and she had had a fascinating career. Born of a poor English family, she had worked her way from chorus girl to top Hollywood columnist. She was bright and spirited and courageous, and she fell in love with him, as he did with her. Sheilah Graham gave him the strength to get through the problems—professional and medical—during his Hollywood years.

Professional problems began when his script for *Three Comrades* was drastically revised by the film's producer, Joseph Mankiewicz. Scott was deeply hurt and wrote Mankiewicz a desperate plea to restore the script to his original version. "I'm a good writer—honest," he pathetically assured him.

Work on his next picture, *Infidelity,* too, went to waste, failing to pass the tough censorship that ruled the movie industry at the time. He was given work, too, on other major films, *Madame Curie* and *The Women,* but his contributions were negligible. Only his life with Sheilah was going well. She gave him courage and love and was able to control his drinking.

This comparatively calm period came to an end when what looked like a promising assignment turned into disaster.

A Hollywood producer named Walter Wanger had hired Budd Schulberg, a young writer, to work on a script for a film dealing with the annual winter carnival at Dartmouth College. Schulberg was a Dartmouth graduate and could supply the background, while Fitzgerald would contribute his professional skills and maturity. When Wanger told Schulberg that Scott Fitzgerald was to work with him, the young writer told him he thought Fitzgerald had died years before. However, he respected Fitzgerald's work and the two men became friends. All went well, until Wanger insisted that the writers actually go to Dartmouth for the winter carnival. Scott had been ill, and Sheilah was so concerned about his making the trip east—she feared a recurrence of the tuberculosis he had fought in Asheville—that she went with him as far as New York. During the plane ride with Schulberg—Sheilah was discreetly sitting in another row—Fitzgerald began to drink, and it was a week before he finally stopped.

His stay at Dartmouth was tragic. The movie company had failed to obtain accommodations for the writers and they had to share a maid's room in the attic of the local hotel. The first night there, they discussed Fitzgerald's novels, and the older writer told Schulberg: "You know, I used to have a beautiful talent once, Baby. It used to be a wonderful feeling to know it was there, and it isn't all gone yet. . . ."

However, from his drunken behavior and disheveled appearance—he was still physically ill—no one at Dartmouth would have known that any of that beautiful talent, that any of the dapper and glamorous Scott Fitzgerald, remained. The once-famous writer, who was supposed to add literary touches to the film, and was supposed to impress Dartmouth's faculty and students, was often incoherent. He seemed to be in a daze as he wandered around the campus aimlessly. One night, reeling with alcohol after a fraternity party, he came face to face with Wanger, who fired him on the spot. On the way back to California, Sheilah saw to it that he was hospitalized for two weeks in New York.

The year 1939 began badly; his contract with MGM was not renewed and after the fiasco at Dartmouth he was given movie work only sporadically. He wrote some short stories and tried unsuccessfully to work on his novel, but he was drinking heavily again. Even Sheilah could no longer cope with the situation. During one drunken rage, he threw a bowl of soup against the wall and threatened to kill her— while he was looking for the gun, she called the police.

Terrified of his tantrums, Sheilah decided to leave him. When she refused to speak to him on the phone, he sent her threatening notes. One day he stole into her apartment and removed a fur coat he had given her. Sheilah was intimidated and angry, but she also felt pity and compassion for a man who had obviously lost control of himself. In addition, she was in love with him.

In the spring of 1939, Scott unpredictably decided to take Zelda on a short trip to Cuba. Their relationship had been a complicated one since he had settled in Hollywood with Sheilah. The marriage as a marriage was over, and they could never recapture what little happiness they had had in the past. On the one hand, Scott was bitter. He wrote to Scottie soon after she left boarding school:

"When I was your age, I lived with a great dream. The dream grew and I learned how to speak of it and make people listen. Then the dream divided one day when I decided to marry your mother after all, even though I knew she was spoiled and meant no good to me. . . . She didn't have the strength for the big stage—sometimes she pretended, and pretended beautifully, but she didn't have it. She was soft when she should have been hard, and hard when she should have been yielding. . . ."

By the time Scottie was in college at Vassar, he was writing her other letters placing the blame for his failures on Zelda. Yet, he continued to feel responsible for her, and to Zelda herself he wrote warm and affectionate letters, telling her what he was doing, showing his concern for her health as well as for Scottie's future well-being. Perhaps the idea of going to Cuba for a holiday was a good one—after they returned home he wrote Zelda that she was *"the finest, loveliest, tenderest, most beautiful person I have ever known."* Yet the trip itself was another disaster, typical of those he had suffered in the past. While watching a professional cockfight, he became enraged at its cruelty and tried to stop it. The Cuban fans took exception to his interference with their sport, and he was mercilessly beaten up. Battered and bruised, he returned to New York where he was once again hospitalized.

Physically and emotionally he seemed to have reached a new low, and he was once again running short of money. Even worse, he had reached the conclusion that all of his friends, with the exception of Maxwell Perkins and Gerald Murphy, had turned against him. Hemingway had reacted unsympathetically to "The Crack-Up" and had made what Fitzgerald considered a snide remark about him in one of his stories, "The Snows of Kilimanjaro." He felt that John Peale Bishop had betrayed him in a published article in which he stated that Fitzgerald had flunked out of Princeton and had spent too much time playing up to the rich. *"It can't be jealousy,"* Scott wrote to Edmund Wilson, with whom he was still on good if less intimate terms, *"for there isn't much to be jealous of any more."* Most serious of all, he broke with his agent and friend Harold Ober. Ober had encouraged and helped Fitzgerald loyally for many years; he and his wife had acted as parents to Scottie during her adolescence. Yet when Ober turned down one of Fitzgerald's requests for money—which he had granted so many times in the past— Fitzgerald angrily turned on him. In the future he would represent himself, without the aid of any agent. *"Once I be-lieved in friendship,"* he wrote to Perkins, *"believed I <u>could</u>*

Fitzgerald and Sheilah in Tijuana, Mexico, early in 1940.

(if I didn't always) make people happy and it was more fun than anything. Now even that seems like a vaudevillian's cheap dream of heaven, a vast minstrel show in which one is the perpetual Bones."

In spite of his increasing bitterness and his broken health, Fitzgerald was once again—as had so often been the case during his lifetime—able to regain control of himself. Back in Hollywood in the summer of 1939, he pleaded with Sheilah to return to him, and she did. He cut down on his drinking and began to think seriously about his novel. He was greatly encouraged when a magazine expressed serious interest in publishing it in installments. Perhaps he really had not been forgotten.

Scottie, too, had grown up into a beautiful, bright, and gay young woman, who was showing an interest in and an aptitude for writing. It was Scottie and his concern for her welfare that had often kept him going, and he was beginning to reap the rewards of the care and attention he had shown her during the difficult years. She had been away from home for long periods—at schools in both France and America—but his illness and Zelda's made this inevitable. He had often been too strict with her, had projected his own personality onto hers by insisting that she excel, but father and daughter enjoyed each other's company and love. *"Your life has been a disappointment, as mine has too,"* he wrote Zelda. *"But we haven't gone through this sweat for nothing. Scottie has got to survive. . . ."*

By the end of October, his spirits were high and he wrote

Scottie a glowing letter, saying he was writing *"something that is maybe great,"* that he felt alive once again. Even his anger at Hollywood had disappeared. *"I'm convinced that maybe they're not going to make me a Czar of the Industry right away, as I thought 10 months ago. It's all right, Baby —life has humbled me—Czar or not, we'll survive. I am even willing to compromise for assistant Czar. . . ."*

The following year, 1940, would, he was sure, be even better. He was aware of the mistakes and mishaps of the past as he summed up twenty years of his life in a letter to Zelda. *"Twenty years ago* This Side of Paradise *was a best seller and we were settled in Westport. Ten years ago Paris was having almost its last great American season but we had quit the gay parade and you were gone to Switzerland. Five years ago I had my first bad stroke of illness and went to Asheville. Cards began falling badly for us much too early."* Yet, absorbed in and excited by his new novel, he felt a new start could be made and a new future built.

The novel, called *The Last Tycoon,* took up almost all of his time. It was a story of Hollywood, of life in one of the great studios and more specifically of a brilliant and dynamic producer and his obsessive love for a mysterious woman. He sent frequent reports to Zelda of his progress. On October 11, he wrote that he had two more months' work ahead of him. A week later, he said that it was like writing *Tender Is the Night,* that he thought of nothing else, that his room was covered with charts, *"telling the different movements of the characters and their histories."* On October 23: *"I am deep*

A self-portrait of Zelda sometime in the early 1940s.

in the novel, living in it, and it makes me happy." November
2: *"The novel is hard as pulling teeth but that is because it
is in its early character-planting phase. I feel people so less
intently than I did once that this is harder. It means welding*

together hundreds of stray impressions and incidents to form the fabric of entire personalities." The following week he reported that the novel was growing under his hand—"*not as deft a hand as I'd like—but growing,*" and two weeks later he wrote Zelda that he was digging it out of himself like uranium.

The Last Tycoon was to be his way to redemption, and he struggled hard to complete it. However, his deteriorating physical condition slowed him down. In early December, he suffered a minor heart attack, which forced him to spend most of his time in bed. He continued to write as much as his strength would allow, using a special wooden desk that he had had made to order at the time of an earlier illness. The doctors reported that the cardiograms showed that his heart was repairing itself, but that it was a slow process.

On December 20, Fitzgerald finished the first part of his sixth chapter after which he and Sheilah went to the movies. On the way out of the theatre, he felt a sharp pain, and a frightened Sheilah had to help him home. She was greatly relieved in the morning when Scott said he felt much better.

After lunch, while awaiting a routine visit from his doctor, he began to read an article about the Princeton football team. When he finished it, he got up from his chair and suddenly fell to the ground. In a matter of minutes, he was dead.

Premature and tragic as it was, F. Scott Fitzgerald's death was at least less torturous than his life had been. A golden-haired youth, with an enormous gift for writing, he had had the whole world before him. As he had written to Zelda, however, the cards had begun falling badly too early. The last decade and a half of his short life—he was only forty-four when he died—were almost unrelieved tragedy. Worse, he died believing that he had failed as a writer.

His final hopes lay in *The Last Tycoon* and when the incompleted version, together with his notes for the rest of the novel (edited by Edmund Wilson), was published many years later, critics felt it might indeed have been his masterpiece. Yet he did not need *The Last Tycoon* to assure him the success he so avidly desired. He is in 1974 one of America's most popular writers, certain of a place among the great American writers of the twentieth century.

Scott Fitzgerald had been buried in the Rockville Union Cemetery outside of Baltimore on December 27, 1940. On March 11, 1947, the sanitarium at Highland, North Carolina, burned down and Zelda, who was on the top floor, was engulfed in flames and died. A few days later she was buried beside her husband, and their fairy tale came to its bitter end.

BOOKS BY F. SCOTT FITZGERALD

Most of Fitzgerald's writing is available, at this time, in paperback editions published by Scribner's Contemporary Classics. Included in this series are the following titles:

This Side of Paradise
Flappers and Philosophers
The Beautiful and Damned
Six Tales of the Jazz Age and Other Stories
The Great Gatsby
Tender Is the Night
Taps at Reveille
The Last Tycoon
Babylon Revisited and Other Stories
The Pat Hobby Stories

In addition, the same series includes two interesting anthologies:

The Stories of F. Scott Fitzgerald, with an introduction by Malcolm Cowley.
The Fitzgerald Reader, edited and with an introduction by Arthur Mizener.

Two essential volumes of Fitzgerald's autobiographical writings, both available in paperback, are:

Afternoon of an Author, edited by Arthur Mizener, Scribner's.
The Crack-Up, edited by Edmund Wilson, New Directions.

FOR FURTHER READING

Any reader interested in learning more about Fitzgerald should read:

The Letters of F. Scott Fitzgerald, edited by Andrew Turnbull and published by Scribner's, New York, in 1963. It is currently available in a paperback edition.

The two most comprehensive biographies of Fitzgerald, also available in paperback, are:

Mizener, Arthur: *The Far Side of Paradise*, Houghton Mifflin, Boston, 1951; revised edition, 1965.

Turnbull, Andrew: *Scott Fitzgerald*, Scribner's, New York, 1962.

Among other books of interest are:

As Ever, Scott Fitzgerald, edited by Matthew J. Bruccoli, Lippincott, Philadelphia, 1972.

Dear Scott/Dear Max; the Fitzgerald-Perkins Correspondence, edited by John Kuehl and Jackson Bryer, Scribner's, New York, 1971.

Eble, Kenneth (ed.): *F. Scott Fitzgerald*, McGraw-Hill, New York, 1973.

Graham, Sheilah, and Frank, Gerold: *Beloved Infidel*, Holt, Rinehart & Winston, New York, 1958.

Kazin, Alfred: *F. Scott Fitzgerald: The Man and His Work*, World, Cleveland and New York, 1951.

Latham, Aaron: *Crazy Sundays: F. Scott Fitzgerald in Hollywood*, Viking, New York, 1970.

Milford, Nancy: *Zelda*, Harper & Row, New York, 1970.

Mizener, Arthur (ed.): *F. Scott Fitzgerald: A Collection of Critical Essays*, Prentice-Hall, Englewood Cliffs, N.J., 1963.

Sklar, Robert: *F. Scott Fitzgerald: The Last Laocoön*, Oxford University Press, New York, 1967.

Tomkins, Calvin: *Living Well Is the Best Revenge*, Viking, New York, 1971.

PHOTOCREDITS

The author wishes to acknowledge for the use of photographs:

The Bettmann Archive, Inc: frontispiece
Bettmann/Springer Film Archive: 47
Culver Pictures: 71, 121
Frances Scott Fitzgerald Smith: 3, 4, 7, 8, 15, 22, 27, 29, 32, 35,
    81, 85, 90, 105, 111, 124
Honoria M. Donnelly: 86
The New York Public Library: 53, 72

INDEX

South Campus
White Bear Lake Area High School
3551 McKnight Road
White Bear Lake, MN 55110